UN MUNDO FELIZ

**PROTEST:
PICTOGRAM
ACTIVISM
TO CHANGE
THE WORLD**

**PROTEST:
PICTOGRAMMES
ET GRAPHISME
POUR CHANGER
LE MONDE**

**PROTESTA:
PICTOGRAMAS
Y GRAFISMO
PARA CAMBIAR
EL MUNDO**

Strajk Kobiet / Krakow and Warsaw

HOAKI

WAR
YES
Política
¡PENSIONES DIGNAS YA!

Key Clues / Indices Clé / Pistas
—

Tea Party
México '68
Otpor!
La Catrina / Unicode
Animal Rights Movement
Occupy / Occuprint
Butterflies (Las Mirabal)
Make Love Not War
PAH
Arab Spring
Ley Mordaza
If I can't dance, I don't want to be part of...
Liberation Theology
Craftivism
Guerrilla Etiquette
#FeesMustFall
Carnation Revolution / Revolução dos Cravos
Combahee River Collective
Nous Sommes le Pouvoir
Girifna
Chicago Women's Graphics Collective
Aidez l'Espagne
El Siluetazo
Artists Against Police Violence
Pussy Galore
The March for Our Lives
March for Peace
Marcha Migrante
Ni Una Menos
Women's Rights Activists
No More Miss America!
I Am an Optical Illusion
Body-poster
See Red Women's Workshop
Movimento delle Sardine
Reclaim the Streets
Unfair Play / Olympukes
Umbrella Revolution
The Smiley / The Smiling Sun
Snow Revolution
Yayoflautas
Amazon
The Graphic Workshop
The God Bless Graffiti Coalition (GBGC)
15-M / Voces con Futura
Gran Fury
Anti-Austerity Activists
Fast Food Nation / Super Size Me
Dirty Protest
Motherfuckers
Safety Pin
People's Climate March
Pictograms to the world
School Strike for Climate
Nuclear Disarmament
The Second Intifada
I Am a Man
Failure is Impossible
Medu Art Ensemble
Stop de Kindermoord
Provo
Heroic Guerrilla Fighter
Sanitarios Necesarios / Salva lo Público
No Blood for Oil
Anti Nazi League

for/pour/para Rini Templeton (1935–1986)
Gerd Arntz (1900–1988)

UN MUNDO FELIZ

iNTRO

LIZ MCQUISTON
—
LONDON
MARCH 16, 2020

We are all used to seeing pictograms in daily life: they direct, they instruct and they represent us in frozen, diagrammatic form. We are told that they are an important element of 'visual language', as they allow us to communicate with each other despite differences in spoken language. But do they? Or are they really just lifeless depictions reminding us of our isolation?

Operating on a completely different level of thinking, Sonia and Gabriel Freeman (Un Mundo Feliz) imbue their pictomontages or 'pictos' with passion, politics and wit. Their pictos scream, they cry, they shout warnings, they laugh (at us? well, of course). And at times they are made of combined symbols that make no immediate sense at all… but we are forced to think, then to wonder, and finally, to go to other places in our minds. When pictos are gathered together in quantity, such as in a book or exhibition, they become an army of ideas and emotions that take us on a politicised journey of doubt – and revelation. The horrible, excitable, fantastic pictos wake us up. They force us to be human, to feel their emotion, to be brave, and then… to take action.

Liz McQuiston
author of Protest! A History of Social and Political Protest Graphics *(2019) and other publications on design and activism*

—

elle est l'auteure de « Protest! A History of Social and Political Protest Graphics » (2019) [Trad. fr.« Rébellion ! Histoire mondiale de l'art contestataire »] et d'autres publications sur l'expression artistique et l'activisme

—

autora de Protest! A History of Social and Political Protest Graphics *(2019) y otras publicaciones sobre diseño y activismo*

ENG

Nous sommes tous désormais accoutumés à voir des pictogrammes dans notre quotidien : ils orientent, informent et nous représentent de manière figée et schématique. Ils constituent, dit-on, un élément important du « langage visuel », car ils nous permettent de communiquer les uns avec les autres, même si nous parlons une langue différente. Mais est-ce le cas ? Ou ne sont-ils en réalité que des représentations sans vie qui nous rappellent notre isolement ?

Opérant à un niveau de pensée complètement différent, Sonia et Gabriel Freeman (Un Mundo Feliz) imprègnent leurs pictomontages ou « pictos » de passion, de messages politiques et d'esprit. Leurs pictos hurlent, pleurent, mettent en garde et rient (¿ de nous ? Oui, bien sûr). Et parfois, ce sont des combinaisons de symboles qui ne prennent pas sens immédiatement… mais nous forcent à réfléchir, à nous poser des questions et, finalement, à aller plus loin dans notre réflexion. Ainsi, lorsqu'un grand nombre de pictos sont rassemblés, sous forme de livre ou d'exposition, ils deviennent une armée d'idées et d'émotions, qui nous entraînent dans un voyage politisé, fait de doutes – et de révélations. Ce sont ces pictos, horribles, enthousiasmants et fantastiques, qui nous réveillent, qui nous obligent à être humains, à ressentir leurs émotions, à être courageux, et ensuite… à agir.

Todos estamos acostumbrados a ver pictogramas en la vida cotidiana: nos dirigen, nos instruyen y nos representan de una forma fría y esquemática. Se nos dice que son un elemento importante del «lenguaje visual», ya que nos permiten comunicarnos entre nosotros a pesar de las diferencias de idioma. ¿Pero lo hacen? ¿O son meras representaciones sin vida que nos recuerdan nuestro aislamiento?

Operando con un enfoque completamente diferente, Sonia y Gabriel Freeman (Un Mundo Feliz) impregnan sus *pictomontajes o pictos* con pasión, ideas políticas e ingenio. Sus pictogramas gritan, lloran, lanzan advertencias, se ríen (¿de nosotros? bueno, por supuesto). Y a veces están hechos de símbolos combinados que no tienen ningún sentido inmediato… pero nos vemos obligados a pensar, luego a maravillarnos y finalmente a ir a otros lugares de nuestra mente. Así, cuando los pictogramas se reúnen en cantidad, como en un libro o una exposición, se convierten en un ejército de ideas y emociones que nos conducen a un viaje politizado de duda y revelación. Los horribles, excitantes y fantásticos pictogramas nos despiertan. Nos obligan a ser humanos, a sentir su emoción, a ser valientes, y luego… a actuar.

THE SEEDS OF REBELLION

LES GRAINES DE LA RÉBELLION

LAS SEMILLAS DE LA REBELIÓN

STEVEN HELLER
—
NEW YORK
APRIL 16, 2020

Steven Heller
*for 33 years he was an art director at
the New York Times. Currently, he is
co-chair of the MFA Designer as Author
Department, Special Consultant to
the President of SVA for New Programs,
and writes the Visuals column for
the New York Times Book Review*
—
*il a été directeur artistique au New York
Times pendant 33 ans. Actuellement,
il co-dirige le Département Arts Graphiques
et Design de la New York School of Visual
Arts et rédige la colonne « Visuals »
de la New York Times Book Review*
—
*durante 33 años fue director de arte
en el* New York Times. *Actualmente
es copresidente del MFA Designer as
Author Department, Consultor Especial
del Presidente de la SVA para Nuevos
Programas, y escribe la columna
de Diseño e Imagen de* New York Times
Book Review

COVID-19 has snuffed out many lives as the pandemic swooshes throughout the world's populations like a monsoon. Viruses are the deadliest microbes: they are hard to control, and difficult to kill. When compared to warfare, I'm not sure which scourge is worse. Actually, neither is less deadly than the other, and one often gives rise to the other. From the early twentieth to the twenty-first century, growing enmity among peoples, races, religions and social classes have provided a steady stream of terror. The deeper we sink into the cesspool of modern existence, the more we see how important it is to have courage and strength to fight against these diseases. We need progressive thinkers and doers who are not afraid to express disgust and anger, to trigger calls to action. We need might to fight might, but we also need symbols of the struggle to instigate struggle.

That is where graphic signs, symbols, posters and other graphics – although only as strong as the paper they are printed on – can have positive effects, at least as motivational and aspirational iconography. Although graphic expression will not change a present or future of pestilence and injustice – and might only serve as a bandage covering a festering sore – it is better to join the chorus of protest than not, if only to show that there is an opposition. Resistance to oppression, prejudice and power usually starts with small things. The protest and cautionary graphics in this book are small things compared to the weaponry of evil, but they are reminders that tyranny is not the norm. There are many individuals in the armies of the righteous who are represented by the signs and symbols, the logos and marks found in this collection – and those used on the streets and in media.

At the risk of overstating the impact of these graphic devices, as a critical mass they speak a certain truth to specific power. They contain the seeds of rebellion. Perhaps this book contains one or more graphic designs that by design or serendipity will be the next peace sign or other visual motif that rallies the world together under a world enhancing banner. Then again, maybe not. But we can hope, right?

ENG
....

COVID-19 a détruit de nombreuses vies ; telle une mousson, la pandémie s'est abattue, et s'abat encore, sur les populations du monde entier. Les virus sont les microbes les plus mortels ; ils sont difficiles à contrôler et à tuer. Comparés à la guerre, j'ignore quel fléau est le plus grave. En fait, aucun des deux n'est moins meurtrier. Et l'un engendre souvent l'autre. Du début du XXe au XXIe siècles, l'inimitié croissante entre les peuples, les races, les religions et les classes sociales a généré un flot ininterrompu de terreur. Plus nous nous enfonçons dans le cloaque de l'existence moderne, plus nous voyons combien il est important d'avoir le courage et la force de lutter contre ces maladies. Nous avons besoin d'acteurs et de penseurs progressistes qui n'aient pas peur d'exprimer leur dégoût et leur colère et de lancer des appels à l'action. Nous avons besoin de force pour lutter contre la force, mais aussi de symboles de lutte pour susciter la lutte.

C'est là que les signes graphiques, les symboles, les affiches et d'autres images - même s'ils ne sont pas plus « résistants » que le papier sur lequel ils sont imprimés - peuvent avoir des effets positifs, du moins en tant qu'iconographie mobilisatrice et stimulante. Bien que l'expression graphique ne changera en rien un présent ou un avenir de pestilence et d'injustice - et peut seulement faire office de pansement pour couvrir une plaie infectée - il vaut mieux se joindre au chœur des protestations que de ne rien faire du tout, ne serait-ce que pour montrer qu'il y a une opposition ! La résistance à l'oppression, aux préjugés et au pouvoir commence généralement par de petites choses. Les images de contestation et de mise en garde de ce livre ne sont qu'un grain de sable, comparées à l'arsenal du mal, mais elles rappellent que la tyrannie n'est pas la norme. Une foule d'individus constituant l'armée des justes sont représentés par les signes et les symboles, les logos et les graffitis de ce recueil - et par ceux qui sont utilisés dans la rue et dans les médias.

Au risque d'exagérer l'impact de ces dispositifs graphiques, en tant que masse critique, ils disent une certaine vérité qui génère de l'énergie. Ils contiennent les germes de la rébellion. Peut-être ce livre contient-il un ou plusieurs dessins graphiques qui, délibérément ou par hasard, seront le prochain signe de paix ou le prochain motif visuel qui ralliera le monde sous la bannière d'un avenir meilleur. Ou peut-être pas. Mais on peut espérer, n'est-ce pas ?

El Covid-19 acabó con muchas vidas mientras la pandemia se extendía por las poblaciones del mundo como un monzón. Los virus son los microbios más mortíferos; son difíciles de controlar y de matar. Comparados con la guerra, no estoy seguro de cuál de los dos flagelos es peor. En realidad, no hay uno que sea menos mortal que el otro. Y, a menudo, uno provoca el otro. Desde principios del siglo xx hasta el siglo XXI, la creciente enemistad entre pueblos, razas, religiones y clases sociales ha generado un flujo constante de terror y cuanto más nos hundimos en el pozo negro de la existencia moderna, más comprendemos la importancia de tener valor y fuerza para luchar contra estas enfermedades. Necesitamos pensadores y hacedores progresistas que no teman expresar su repugnancia y su ira, y que desencadenen llamadas a la acción. Necesitamos fuerza para luchar contra la fuerza, pero también símbolos de lucha para instigar la lucha.

Es ahí donde los signos gráficos, símbolos, carteles y otras formas gráficas —aunque sólo sean tan fuertes como el papel en el que están impresos— pueden tener efectos positivos, al menos como una iconografía deseable y motivadora. Aunque la expresión gráfica no cambiara el presente ni el futuro de pestilencia e injusticia y sólo sirviera como una venda para cubrir una llaga infectada, es mejor unirse al coro de la protesta —aunque sólo sea para mostrar que hay una oposición— que no hacerlo. La resistencia a la opresión, a los prejuicios y al poder suele empezar con cosas pequeñas. La protesta y las advertencias gráficas de este libro son insignificantes comparadas con el armamento del mal, pero son un recordatorio de que la tiranía no es la norma. En los ejércitos de los justos hay muchos individuos que están representados por los signos y símbolos, los emblemas y marcas que se encuentran en esta colección y que se usan en las calles y en los medios de comunicación.

A riesgo de exagerar el impacto de estos dispositivos gráficos, sumados declaran una verdad incuestionable a un poder específico. Contienen las semillas de la rebelión. Tal vez este libro incluya uno o más diseños que, por inspiración o casualidad, sean el próximo símbolo de la paz u otro motivo visual que reúna al mundo bajo un estandarte que lo realce. O quizás no. Aunque podemos tener esa esperanza, ¿verdad?

RECLAIM THE STREETS — CLAIM ANOTHER WORLD

RECONQUÉRIR LES RUES — REVENDIQUER UN AUTRE MONDE

RECUPERAR LAS CALLES — REIVINDICAR OTRO MUNDO

BETTINA RICHTER
—
ZÜRICH
3 JUNE, 2020

Bettina Richter
*is an art historian who studied in
Heidelberg, Paris, and Zurich. From 1997
to 2006, she served as a research associate
in the Poster Collection of the Museum für
Gestaltung Zürich, and since 2006 as its
curator and the editor of the publication
series 'Poster Collection'. She also lectures
at the Zürcher Hochschule der Künste
and works as a freelance writer. She has
published articles and essays on art history,
literature, and posters*
—
*elle est historienne de l'art et a étudié à
Heidelberg, Paris et Zurich. De 1997 à
2006, elle a travaillé en tant qu'associée
de recherche dans la collection d'affiches
du Museum für Gestaltung Zürich et, depuis
2006, elle est la conservatrice et l'éditrice
de la série de publications « Poster Collection ».
Elle enseigne également à la Zürcher
Hochschule der Künste et travaille comme
écrivain indépendante. Elle a publié des
articles et des essais sur l'histoire de l'art,
la littérature et les affiches*
—
*es historiadora del arte y estudió en
Heidelberg, París y Zürich. De 1997 a
2006, trabajó como investigadora asociada
en la colección de carteles del Museum
für Gestaltung Zürich, y desde 2006
como comisaria y editora de la serie de
publicaciones «Poster Collection». También
da clases en la Zürcher Hochschule der
Künste, es escritora independiente y
ha publicado artículos y ensayos sobre
historia del arte, literatura y cartelismo*

In these times of COVID-19, social distancing is often a welcome argument for banning demonstrations. But visual cries cannot be banned or banished from public space. Posters, flyers, and stickers remind us that not only viruses kill, but also borders. That care work, suddenly recognized as systemically relevant, has always been done by underpaid women. That a pandemic is not a stroke of fate but is due to destructive human interaction with nature.

Graphics have great activist potential. Social media did not establish this quality, it has only reinforced it. They are cost-effective, easy to reproduce, easy to distribute, unmistakable, immediate, in the best cases universally understandable, timely, and timeless, all at once. El' Lissitzky, John Heartfield, Käthe Kollwitz, Atelier Populaire, Shigeo Fukuda, Luba Lukova, David Tartakover, James Victore, and many others: all are fighters, whether with the drawing pencil or with today's abundant technological aids. Un Mundo Feliz, with their images condensed into symbols, is part of this tradition. Their inventory of pictograms is a powerful counter-design to a world view of capitalist logos. It is a visual memory of resistance movements worldwide. Playing with wit, poetry, and ambiguity, the pictograms continue to be an invitation to joyful self-empowerment, to resistance. And this – according to German writer Peter Weiss in his epochal work – fundamentally requires an aesthetics to be and remain effective. Creative power and passionate commitment are not a bad place to start.

In the USA, the streets are currently bleeding again, despite Corona. The Black Lives Matter movement, the people are not allowing their cries to be banned. Nor are they allowing their uprising and solidarity against racist murders by the police and state-sanctioned violence against the colonized body to be put down. That these cries may not die away, that they echo globally and remain in memory: the graphic designs of Un Mundo Feliz contribute to this.

ENG

En ces temps de COVID-19, la distanciation sociale est souvent un argument de poids pour interdire les manifestations. Mais les cris visuels ne peuvent pas être interdits ou bannis de l'espace public. Des affiches, des dépliants et des autocollants nous rappellent que non seulement les virus mais aussi les frontières tuent. Ce travail de soins, dont on reconnaît soudainement l'importance systémique, a toujours été effectué par des femmes sous-payées. Qu'une pandémie n'est pas un coup du sort, mais qu'elle est due à une interaction humaine destructrice avec la nature.

Les signes graphiques ont un énorme potentiel militant. Les réseaux sociaux n'ont pas établi cette qualité, ils l'ont seulement renforcée. Rentables, faciles à reproduire et à distribuer, sans équivoque, immédiats, dans le meilleur des cas, universellement compréhensibles, actuels et intemporels tout à la fois. El' Lissitzky, John Heartfield, Käthe Kollwitz, Atelier Populaire, Shigeo Fukuda, Luba Lukova, David Tartakover ou James Victore et bien d'autres : tous sont des combattants, que ce soit avec leur crayon en main ou grâce aux nombreux moyens techniques d'aujourd'hui. Avec ses images condensées en symboles, Un Mundo Feliz s'inscrit dans cette tradition. Son inventaire de pictogrammes est un puissant contre-projet à la vision du monde des logos capitalistes. C'est une mémoire visuelle des mouvements de résistance dans le monde. Jouant avec l'esprit, la poésie et l'ambiguïté, les pictogrammes ne cessent d'être une invitation à une joyeuse autonomisation, à la résistance. Et cela - selon l'écrivain allemand Peter Weiss dans son œuvre marquante - exige fondamentalement une esthétique pour être et rester efficace. Le pouvoir créatif et l'engagement passionné ne sont pas un mauvais point de départ.

Aux États-Unis, les rues saignent à nouveau, malgré le coronavirus. Le mouvement Black Lives Matter, les gens n'admettent pas que leurs cris soient interdits. Ils ne permettent pas non plus que leur soulèvement et leur solidarité contre les meurtres racistes, commis par la police, et la violence sanctionnée par l'État contre les minorités colonisées soient réprimés. Que ces cris ne faiblissent pas, qu'ils résonnent dans le monde entier et restent dans nos mémoires : Le graphisme de Un Mundo Feliz y contribue.

En tiempos del Covid-19, el distanciamiento social ha sido a menudo un argumento de peso para impedir las manifestaciones. Pero los gritos visuales no pueden ser prohibidos ni desterrados del espacio público. Los carteles, *flyers* y pegatinas nos recuerdan que no sólo los virus matan sino también las fronteras. Que el trabajo de *cuidar*, reconocido inesperadamente como importante, siempre ha sido realizado por mujeres mal pagadas. Que una pandemia no es un golpe del destino, sino el fruto de la interacción destructiva del hombre con la naturaleza.

El grafismo tiene un gran potencial activista. Los medios de comunicación social se han limitado a reforzar esta cualidad, no la han justificado. Rentable, fácil de reproducir, sencillo de distribuir, inconfundible, inmediato, en muchos casos universalmente comprensible; oportuno y atemporal a la vez. El' Lissitzky, John Heartfield, Käthe Kollwitz, Atelier Populaire, Shigeo Fukuda, Luba Lukova, David Tartakover, James Victore y muchos otros: todos ellos son luchadores armados con el lápiz de dibujo o con los medios tecnológicos de hoy en día. Un Mundo Feliz, con sus imágenes condensadas en símbolos, forma parte de esta tradición. Su inventario de pictogramas es un poderoso contradiseño del enfoque mundial de los logos capitalistas. Es un archivo sin palabras de los movimientos de resistencia en todo el mundo. Jugando con el ingenio, la poesía y la ambigüedad, los pictogramas son siempre una invitación al empoderamiento gozoso, a la resistencia. Y ésta —según destaca el escritor alemán Peter Weiss en su gran obra— necesita una estética para ser y permanecer efectiva. El poder creativo y el compromiso apasionado no son malos requisitos para conseguirla.

En los EE.UU. las calles están sangrando de nuevo a pesar del coronavirus. *Black Live Matters*, la gente no permite que se le prohíba alzar su clamor, ni el levantamiento común en solidaridad contra los asesinatos racistas de la policía y la violencia contra los cuerpos colonizados sancionada por el Estado. Que estos gritos no se desvanezcan, que encuentren un eco global y permanezcan en la memoria: el diseño gráfico de Un Mundo Feliz contribuye a que eso suceda.

FR

ES

THE REV☠LUTI☠NARY SïGN

LE SïGNE RÉV☠LUTï☠NNAïRE

EL SïGN☠ REV☠LUCï☠NARï☠

EXPERIMENTAL JETSET

—

AMSTERDAM
APRIL 26, 2020

Experimental Jetset
is a small, independent, Amsterdam-based graphic design studio, founded in 1997 by (and still consisting of) Marieke Stolk, Erwin Brinkers, and Danny van den Dungen. Focusing on printed matter and site-specific installations, and describing their methodology as 'turning language into objects', Experimental Jetset have worked on projects for a wide variety of institutes
—
c'est un petit studio indépendant de graphisme, créé en 1997 à Amsterdam par (et toujours composé de) Marieke Stolk, Erwin Brinkers et Danny van den Dungen. Privilégiant la matière imprimée et les installations in situ et décrivant sa méthode comme « la transformation du langage en objets », Experimental Jetset a travaillé sur des projets pour de nombreux instituts
—
es un estudio de diseño gráfico, pequeño e independiente, con sede en Ámsterdam, fundado en 1997 (y todavía compuesto) por Marieke Stolk, Erwin Brinkers y Danny van den Dungen. Se centra en el diseño impreso y las instalaciones en sitios específicos y, siguiendo su metodología de «convertir el lenguaje en objetos», ha trabajado en proyectos para una amplia variedad de instituciones

In his manifesto 'Anti-Tendenz Kunst' ('Against Engaged Art', 1923), Theo van Doesburg states that 'there is no fundamental difference between a portrait of Napoleon and a portrait of Trotsky' – no matter how revolutionary the subject, it is the notion of portraiture itself that will render the painting bourgeois. In his essay 'The Aesthetic Dimension' (1977), Herbert Marcuse suggests something similar – it is not the message that makes a work of art revolutionary, but the way in which that message is delivered. And we tend to agree.

To revolve is to turn – and thus, a revolutionary sign should always turn towards (and into) itself, reflecting on its own function as a sign, revealing its own materiality, deconstructing its own message. Critical propaganda should first and foremost be critical of itself, sabotaging its own strategies, denouncing its own authority. Further, the word 'activist' in 'activist art' should not refer to the activism of the artist, but to the ability of art to activate the viewer – encouraging the viewer not to consume a message in a passive way, but instead to engage with the piece of art in an active way. The goal shouldn't be to change opinions, but to radically change ways of seeing and thinking.

A revolutionary sign should be able to push and pull at the same time – it should deliver a message, while at the same time destabilizing the path of delivery. It should be both a sign and an anti-sign. The sign should be designed, and de-signed.

ENG

Dans son manifeste « Anti-Tendenz Kunst », Theo van Doesburg affirme qu' « il n'y a pas de différence fondamentale entre un portrait de Napoléon et un portrait de Trotsky » - aussi révolutionnaire que soit le sujet, c'est la notion de portrait en soi qui rendra le tableau bourgeois. Dans son essai « The Aesthetic Dimension » (1977) [Trad. fr. « La dimension esthétique » (1978)], Herbert Marcuse suggère quelque chose de similaire : ce n'est pas le message qui rend une œuvre d'art révolutionnaire, mais la manière dont ce message est transmis. Et nous tendons à être d'accord.

Revolver, c'est tourner – et, donc, un signe révolutionnaire[1] devrait toujours se tourner vers (et en) lui-même, en réfléchissant sur sa propre fonction de signe, en révélant sa propre matérialité, en déconstruisant son propre message. La propagande critique doit avant tout être critique envers elle-même, en sabotant ses propres stratégies et en dénonçant sa propre autorité. En outre, le mot « activiste » dans « art activiste » ne doit pas faire référence à l'activisme de l'artiste, mais à la capacité de l'art à mobiliser le spectateur - en l'encourageant à ne pas consommer un message passivement, mais plutôt à s'engager activement avec l'œuvre d'art. L'objectif ne devrait pas être de changer les opinions, mais de changer radicalement la façon de voir et de penser.

Un signe révolutionnaire doit pouvoir pousser et tirer en même temps - il doit délivrer un message, tout en déstabilisant le chemin de la diffusion. Il doit être à la fois un signe et un anti-signe. Le *sign* doit être designed et *de-signed*.[2]

En su manifiesto *Anti-Tendenz Kunst* («Contra el arte comprometido», 1923), Theo van Doesburg afirma que «no hay ninguna diferencia fundamental entre un retrato de Napoleón y un retrato de Trotsky»: no importa cuan revolucionario sea el tema, es la noción del retrato en sí la que hará que la pintura sea burguesa. En su ensayo *La dimensión estética* (1977), Herbert Marcuse sugiere algo similar: no es el mensaje lo que hace revolucionaria una obra de arte, sino la forma en que se transmite ese mensaje. Y tendemos a estar de acuerdo con ellos.

Revolver es girar; por lo tanto, un signo revolucionario[1] debe siempre volverse hacia (y dentro de) sí mismo, reflexionando sobre su propia función como signo, revelando su propia materialidad, deconstruyendo su propio mensaje. La propaganda crítica debe ser ante todo crítica consigo misma, saboteando sus propias estrategias, denunciando su propia autoridad. Y la palabra *activista* en la expresión *arte activista* no debería referirse al activismo del artista, sino a la capacidad del arte para activar al espectador, animándolo a no consumir un mensaje de forma pasiva, sino a comprometerse con la obra de arte de forma activa. El objetivo no debería ser cambiar las opiniones, sino cambiar radicalmente la forma de ver y pensar.

Un signo revolucionario debe ser capaz de empujar y tirar al mismo tiempo: debe entregar un mensaje mientras que a la vez desestabiliza la forma de entrega. Debería ser tanto un *sign* como un *non-sign*. El *sign* debe ser *designed* y *de-signed*.[2]

---

1   Le mot « révolution » vient du latin *revolutio* et signifie « action et effet de tourner d'un côté à l'autre ». Ses composantes lexicales sont : le préfixe re- (exprime un mouvement d'inversion), *volvere* (tourner), plus le suffixe -tion (action et effet).
2   *to design* signifie construire, *to de-sign* déconstruire.

1   La palabra *revolución* viene del latín *revolutio* y significa «acción y efecto de dar vuelta de un lado a otro». Sus componentes léxicos son: el prefijo re- («hacia atrás»), *volvere* («dar vueltas»), más el sufijo -ció n («acción y efecto»)
2   Mientras que *to design* significa «construir», *to de-sign* significa «deconstruir»

RAGE CASTS A SHADOW

LA RAGE PROJETTE UNE OMBRE

LA RABIA PROYECTA UNA SOMBRA

AVRAM FINKELSTEIN
—
BROOKLYN, NY
MAY 8, 2020

In our twenty-first century image culture, images are a power vernacular. They provide short cuts to the commons, where narratives are turf. Images define the borders of this turf, through symbols, signifiers, and codes. But to assert relevance, the codes need to remain in constant flux.

For instance, the rainbow flag was once a potent set of codes, but it has become corporate-speak for a marketable form of intersectionality. It used to represent liberation, but now it represents assimilation, and assimilation is the not logical endpoint of liberation. Assimilation is a fantasia of privilege, which is the opposite of liberation. Rage is what drives liberation, and rage casts a shadow. The shadow is resistance.

Avram Finkelstein
is an artist, activist, and writer living in Brooklyn, and a founding member of the Silence=Death and Gran Fury collectives. He is featured in the artist oral history project at the Smithsonian's Archives of American Art. His book, After Silence: A History of AIDS Through its Images, *is available through University of California Press*

—

c'est un artiste, militant et écrivain vivant à Brooklyn et un des membres fondateurs des collectifs Silence=Death et Gran Fury. Il apparaît dans le projet d'histoire orale des artistes aux Archives of American Art de la Smithsonian Institution. Son livre, « After Silence : A History of AIDS Through its Images », *est disponible auprès de l'University of California Press*

—

es un artista, activista y escritor que vive en Brooklyn; es miembro fundador de los colectivos Silence=Death y Gran Fury y aparece en el proyecto de historia oral del artista en los Archivos de Arte Americano del Smithsonian. Su libro, After Silence: A History of AIDS Through its Images, *está disponible en University of California Press*

ENG
....

Dans notre culture de l'image du XXIe siècle, les images sont un pouvoir vernaculaire. Elles proposent des raccourcis vers les espaces communaux, où les récits sont le gazon. Les images définissent les frontières de ce territoire, à travers des symboles, des signifiants et des codes. Mais pour affirmer leur pertinence, les codes doivent rester en évolution constante.

Par exemple, le drapeau arc-en-ciel était autrefois un puissant ensemble de codes, mais il est devenu le jargon corporatiste d'une forme commercialisable d'intersectionnalité. Avant, il représentait la libération, mais aujourd'hui il représente l'assimilation, et l'assimilation est l'aboutissement non logique de la libération. L'assimilation est une illusion de privilège, qui est l'opposé de la libération. La rage est le moteur de la libération et la rage projette une ombre. L'ombre, c'est la résistance.

En nuestra cultura de la imagen del siglo XXI, las imágenes son un poder autóctono. Proporcionan atajos a los bienes comunes, donde las narraciones son territoriales. Las imágenes definen los límites de este territorio, a través de símbolos, significantes y códigos. Pero para tener relevancia, los códigos deben permanecer en constante flujo.

Por ejemplo, la bandera del arco iris fue una vez un potente conjunto de códigos, pero se ha convertido en el lenguaje corporativo de una forma comercial de interseccionalidad. Solía representar la liberación, pero ahora simboliza la asimilación, y la asimilación es el punto final no lógico de la liberación. La asimilación es una fantasía de privilegio, que es lo opuesto a la liberación. La rabia es lo que impulsa la liberación, y la rabia proyecta una sombra. La sombra es la resistencia.

RAGE IS WHAT DRIVES LIBERATION, AND RAGE CASTS A SHADOW. THE SHADOW IS RESISTANCE

AN EXERCISE IN MINDFUL ACTIVISM*

UN EXERCICE D'ACTIVISME CONSCIENT*

UN EJERCICIO DE ACTIVISMO CONSCIENTE*

SARAH CORBETT

—

MAY 11, 2020

A few years ago, I visited a small commercial gallery in York, UK. Politically-charged contemporary art was being exhibited, including a painting of Donald Trump's head in the shape of a cartoon-style bomb. Five prints of this painting were available to buy. I quietly asked the gallery owner how many of the prints he had sold. 'Four,' he replied. And did he know if the buyers were pro- or anti-Trump? He said confidently that two buyers were Trump supporters and two were against Trump's politics.

This story is a reminder to me that 'protest images' are a brilliant opportunity for mindfulness – always helpful in any activism we do. Being aware, without judgement, of what immediate feelings we have towards the image in front of us: are they positive or negative emotions? What do we presume the image is trying to tell us? What baggage or prejudice are we bringing to the image and would we interpret the image differently if we were in a different mood, context, or even time of day? Then looking at the image through the eyes of someone from the completely opposite political ideology we have – do we keep the same understanding or is our response different? If we were of a different gender, race, faith, or age, would we see and feel something different in this image?

Coming to any protest image with a 'beginner's mind' not only helps us reflect more critically about the power of protest imagery, it can also be a personally transformative exercise on the road to being an effective, empathetic part of making the positive change we wish to see in our troubled world.

Sarah Corbett
*award-winning activist, Ashoka Fellow,
and author of* How to Be a Craftivist:
The Art of Gentle Protest (2017).
*She is Founding Director of the Craftivist
Collective and is currently creating*
The Home of Gentle Protest

—

*activiste primée, Ashoka Fellow et auteur
de « How To Be A Craftivist: the art of
gentle protest (2017) ». Directrice fondatrice
du Craftivist Collective et créatrice actuelle
de « The Home of Gentle Protest »*

*activista galardonada, becaria Ashoka y
autora de* How To Be A Craftivist: the art of
gentle protest (2017). *Directora fundadora
del Craftivist Collective y actualmente
creadora de The Home of Gentle Protest*

* *Mindful activism* connects our hands and hearts with our heads giving us the courage to grapple with big issues through deep contemplation

ENG

Il y a quelques années, j'ai visité une petite galerie commerciale à York, au Royaume-Uni. On y exposait de l'art contemporain politiquement engagé, dont un tableau de la tête de Donald Trump en forme de bombe, style dessin animé. Cinq tirages de cette oeuvre étaient en vente. J'ai discrètement demandé au propriétaire de la galerie combien de tirages il avait vendus. « Quatre », m'a-t-il répondu. Et savait-il si les acheteurs étaient pro ou anti Trump ? Il a répondu avec assurance que deux des acheteurs étaient partisans de Trump et les deux autres étaient contre la politique de Trump.

L'histoire me rappelle que les « images contestataires » présentent une formidable occasion d'éveiller les consciences, ce qui est toujours utile dans nos actions militantes. Être conscients, sans jugement, des sentiments immédiats que nous éprouvons face à l'image qu'on a sous les yeux : S'agit-il d'émotions positives ou négatives ? Que peut-on supposer que l'image essaie de nous dire ? Quel bagage ou préjugé apporte-t-on à l'image et interpréterait-on l'image autrement si on était dans un état d'esprit, un contexte, voire un moment de la journée différents ? Puis, si on essaie de regarder l'image à travers les yeux d'une personne dont l'idéologie politique est totalement opposée à la nôtre, aurait-on la même compréhension ou notre réponse serait-elle différente ? Si nous étions d'un sexe, d'une race ou d'un âge différents, verrions-nous et ressentirions-nous quelque chose de différent dans cette image ?

L'approche de ce type d'image avec un « esprit de novice » nous aide non seulement à réfléchir de manière plus critique sur le pouvoir de l'iconographie de la contestation, mais peut également être un exercice de transformation personnelle, visant à faire de nous un élément efficace et empathique participant au changement positif que nous souhaitons voir dans notre monde troublé.

Hace unos años visité una pequeña galería comercial en York (Reino Unido). Se exhibía arte contemporáneo con carga política, y la exposición incluía una obra con la cabeza de Donald Trump en forma de una bomba estilo cómic. Cinco reproducciones de esta imagen estaban a la venta. Pregunté con discreción al dueño de la galería cuántos ejemplares había vendido. «Cuatro», respondió. Le pregunté si sabía si los compradores estaban a favor o en contra de Trump: señaló con toda certeza que dos compradores eran partidarios de Trump y dos estaban en contra de su política.

Esta historia me recuerda que las «imágenes de protesta» son una brillante oportunidad para la toma de conciencia y siempre ayudan en cualquier activismo que hagamos. Ser conscientes, sin juzgar, de los sentimientos inmediatos que experimentamos respecto a la imagen que tenemos delante: ¿son emociones positivas o negativas? ¿Qué suponemos que trata de decirnos la imagen? ¿Qué bagaje o prejuicio le estamos aportando? ¿La interpretaríamos de manera diferente si estuviéramos en otro estado de ánimo, en otro contexto o incluso a una hora diferente del día? Si miráramos la imagen a través de los ojos de alguien de una ideología política completamente opuesta a la nuestra, ¿mantendríamos la misma interpretación, o nuestra respuesta sería distinta? Si fuéramos de un género, raza, fe o edad diferentes, ¿veríamos y sentiríamos algo distinto en esta imagen?

Acercarse a cualquier imagen de protesta con una «mente de aprendiz» no sólo nos ayuda a reflexionar más críticamente sobre el poder de la imaginería de protesta, sino que también puede resultar un ejercicio de transformación personal para llegar a ser una parte efectiva y empática en el logro del cambio positivo que deseamos ver en nuestro problemático mundo.

---

*   *L'activisme conscient* relie nos mains
    et nos cœurs à nos têtes, en nous donnant
    le courage de nous attaquer aux grands
    problèmes grâce à une profonde contemplation.

*   El *activismo consciente* conecta nuestras manos
    y corazones con nuestras cabezas, dándonos
    el valor para afrontar los grandes retos
    a través de una contemplación profunda

FR

ES

LET'S WRITE HUTOPIA

ÉCRIVONS HUTOPIA

ESCRIBAMOS HUTOPIA

ALEJANDRO MAGALLANES
—
CIUDAD DE MÉXICO
MAY 12, 2020

Alejandro Magallanes
is a graphic designer born in Mexico City. He plays with letters and images, sometimes commissioned by someone and sometimes just for fun. To date, he has written seven books and drawn, painted, assembled, and designed many other books, posters, animations, collages, photos, letters, and images. His work has been featured in many exhibitions and has garnered many national and international awards. He is a member of the International Graphic Alliance (AGI)
—

graphiste, né à Mexico. Il joue avec les lettres et les images pour créer des œuvres, qui sont parfois des commandes ou tout simplement pour s'amuser. À ce jour, il a écrit sept livres et a dessiné, peint, assemblé et conçu de nombreux autres livres, affiches, animations, collages, photos, lettres et images. Son travail a fait l'objet de nombreuses expositions et a reçu de nombreux prix nationaux et internationaux. Il est membre de l'Alliance Graphique Internationale (AGI)

diseñador gráfico nacido en la Ciudad de México. Se dedica a jugar con letras e imágenes, a veces encargadas por alguien y otras tan sólo por puro gusto. A la fecha ha escrito siete libros y dibujado, pintado, armado y diseñado muchos otros libros, carteles, animaciones, collages, fotos, letras e imágenes. Ha tenido muchas exposiciones y muchos reconocimientos nacionales e internacionales y es miembro de la Alianza Gráfica Internacional (AGI)

They imagined it, they already intuited it,
    and they thought it,
closed streets and scared people
walking and we make a ditch: a pit
watching instagram, 'twitte and 'feis, buk,
series, ig 'sto:riz, 'podka:sts and zu:mz,
on the left on the right to the left to the right oops!
'stikez, memes and infographics
connected watching netflix and bombings online
and whatsapp group discussions,
I will google democracy
grae'fi:ti your sma:t feun
it's not the same it's the same
the cold war than the war cold
grab a picture make a picture
think and change
thinge and chank
I send these words by dzi:meil
let's write hutopia
so that it shows
a
bra
ve
new
wo
rld

Ils l'ont imaginé, ils l'ont déjà pressenti
    et ils l'ont pensé,
les rues fermées et les gens effrayés
qui marchent et nous faisons un sillon : une fosse
en consultant instagram, tuiter et fessbouc,
série, xtoris, podcas et zoum,
à gauche à droite de la gauchede la droite Allah,
stikers, mèmes et infografie
connectés en regardant netflix et les
bombardements en ligne
et les discussions des groupes watsap,
Je vais chercher la démocratie sur Google
graffiti sur votre smartfone
ce n'est pas la même chose c'est la même chose
la guerre froide que la guerre froide,
prendre une photo faire une photo
penser et changer
penger et chenser
j'envoie ces mots par imèl
écrivons hutopia
pour qu'apparaisse
un
mon
de
heu
reux

ENG / FR

Lo imaginaban, ya lo intuían, y lo pensaban,
las calles cerradas y la gente con miedo
caminando y hacemos un surco: una fosa
viendo instagram, tuiter y feisbuc,
series, estoris, podcases y zumes,
a la izquierda a la derecha de la izquierda
                              de la derecha alá
estiquers, memes e infografías
conectados viendo netflix y bombardeos on line
y discusiones en grupos de guasap,
buscaré democracia en google
grafitea tu esmartfon
no es lo mismo es lo mismo
la guerra fría que la fría guerra
asir una imagen hacer una imagen
pensar y cambiar
pembiar y cansar
mando estas palabras por yimeil
escribamos hutopía
para que se note

                    un
              mun

                        do

            fe

                        liz

PLEASE HELP Y☠URSELF!

SERVEZ-V☠US !

¡P☠R FAV☠R, S☠RVASE!

THOMAS LEMAHIEU
—
MAY 3, 2020

We started out not knowing where we were going. My newspaper, *L'Humanité*, agreed to open a page for graphic designers for a few days, or maybe more. There was just one idea: to reweave that worn-out thread in France, fifty years after May 1968. To remake an Atelier Populaire, in a way, but stateless, without a place, alas, for meetings and exchanges. We wanted to pull the rope, as it were: in '68, the daily paper of the Communist Party had been able, despite ideological differences, to give stocks of paper to the Fine Arts students and especially to the Arts Décos. In short, *'tenir l'affiche'* ('to carry the banner'). This French expression was used as the title of a graphic series which, in the end, will last for two months, from the end of April to the end of June 2018, totaling some fifty publications.* Sonia and Gabriel, from Un Mundo Feliz, participated through Sébastien Marchal. They then went a step further by making an exhibition in Madrid as well as a fanzine in October-November 2018. I'm telling this story because, for me, that's what Un Mundo Feliz is all about: beyond the simple and sharp forms - these never tautological pictographs -, a prolific and overflowing energy flows from them that, in fact, calls to mind the momentum of the Ateliers Populaires and, later on, of Grapus. We have to try our best; though we might make mistakes, let's not be overcautious. Like others elsewhere, the images of Un Mundo Feliz do not impose themselves as works, but induce a relationship, a journey, and a sharing. '68 is not dead. Nothing is finished, there is still more to do. And we need to stay happy, because we will need happiness more than ever to overturn the disorder of this world and prevent a return to the abnormal. Please, help yourself!

Thomas Lemahieu
was born in Liege, Belgium in 1973.
He has been a journalist with the French
daily L'Humanité *since 1998, a major*
reporter for the Monde section, and is host
of the humaginaire.net blog. He is also
a member of the Ne Pas Plier collective

—

né à Liège (Belgique) en 1973, il est
journaliste au quotidien français
« L'Humanité » depuis 1998, grand
reporter à la rubrique Monde et hébergeur
du blog humaginaire.net. Également
membre du collectif Ne Pas Plier

—

nació en Lieja, Bélgica en 1973, periodista
del diario francés L'Humanité *desde 1998,*
destacado reportero de la sección Monde
y promotor del blog humaginaire.net.
Es miembro del colectivo Ne Pas Plier

***   171 canons, Au fond à gauche, Edmond Baudoin, Flora Beillouin, Hélène Bernadat, Valentin Bigel, Clément Boudin, Mustapha Boutadjine, Philippe Bretelle, Bruno Charzat, Pascal Colrat, Bérengère Desmettre, Noel Douglas, Dugudus, Gilles Dupuis, El Fantasma de Heredia, Mohamed Guiga, Isabelle Jégo, Alex Jordan, Raouf Karray, Alain Le Quernec, Kevin Yuen Kit Lo, Sébastien Marchal, Tomaso Marcolla, Josh MacPhee, François Miehe, Ne Rougissez Pas !, Nous Travaillons Ensemble, Daniel Paris-Clavel, Gérard Paris-Clavel, Olivier Pasquiers, Cisco Perez, Caroline Pottier et le Phare Boréal, Fabrice Praeger, Michel Quarez, Collectif La Rage, Thomas Rochon, Jean-Pol Rouard, Thierry Sarfis, Boris Séméniako, Emilie Seto, Fred Sochard, Spark Poster Collective, Super Terrain, Jana Traboulsi, Un Mundo Feliz, Clément Valette, Nicolas Vieira, Atelier Youpi.

ENG

Au début, nous ne savions pas où nous allions. Mon journal, *L'Humanité*, a accepté d'ouvrir une page pour les graphistes pendant quelques jours, ou peut-être plus. Il n'y avait qu'une idée : retisser ce lien usé en France, cinquante ans après mai 68. Refaire un Atelier Populaire, en quelque sort, mais apatride et, malheureusement, sans lieu de rencontres et d'échanges. Nous voulions, si je puis dire, tirer sur la corde : en 68, le quotidien du Parti communiste avait pu, malgré les différences idéologiques, donner des stocks de papier aux étudiants des Beaux-Arts et surtout des Arts Décos. En bref, *tenir l'affiche*. Cette expression a servi de titre à une série graphique qui, au bout du compte, a duré deux mois, de fin avril à fin juin 2018, avec au total une cinquantaine de publications.* Sonia et Gabriel, d'Un Mundo Feliz, y ont participé par l'intermédiaire de Sébastien Marchal. Ils sont ensuite allés plus loin en réalisant une exposition à Madrid ainsi qu'un fanzine en octobre-novembre 2018. Je raconte cette histoire parce que, selon moi, c'est ça, Un Mundo Feliz : au-delà des formes simples et incisives, il se dégage de ces pictogrammes - qui ne sont jamais tautologiques - une énergie prolifique et débordante qui, en fait, rappelle la dynamique des Ateliers Populaires et, ensuite, celui de Grapus. Nous devons faire de notre mieux ; même si nous risquons de faire des erreurs, ne soyons pas trop frileux. Comme d'autres ailleurs, les images de Un Mundo Feliz ne s'imposent pas en tant qu'œuvres, mais elles incitent à une relation, un cheminement, un partage. 68 n'est pas mort. Rien n'est achevé, il reste encore à faire. Et nous devons continuer à nous réjouir, car nous allons avoir plus que jamais besoin de bonheur pour renverser le désordre de ce monde et empêcher un retour à l'anormal. Je vous en prie, servez-vous !

Empezamos sin saber adónde íbamos. Mi periódico, *L'Humanité*, aceptó abrir una página para diseñadores gráficos por unos días, o más. Sólo había una idea: volver a tejer el hilo desgastado en Francia, cincuenta años después de mayo de 1968. Rehacer un Atelier Populaire, de alguna manera, pero apátrida, sin un lugar —por desgracia— para reuniones e intercambios. Tirando de la cuerda: la vida cotidiana del Partido Comunista había sido capaz, a pesar de las diferencias ideológicas, de dar montañas de papel a los estudiantes de las Bellas Artes y especialmente de las Artes Decorativas. En resumen, para *tenir l'affiche*. Esta expresión francesa se utilizó como título de una serie gráfica que, en definitiva, duraría dos meses, desde finales de abril hasta finales de junio de 2018, con unas cincuenta publicaciones.* Sonia y Gabriel, de Un Mundo Feliz, participaron a través de Sébastien Marchal. Luego fueron más allá e hicieron una exposición en Madrid así como un fanzine en octubre-noviembre de 2018. Cuento esta historia porque, para mí, eso es Un Mundo Feliz, más allá de las formas simples y agudas, estos pictogramas nunca tautológicos: una energía prolífica y desbordante que, de hecho, se refiere al impulso de los Ateliers Populaires y, más tarde, de Grapus. Tenemos que intentarlo, es posible que cometamos errores, pero no seamos demasiado precavidos. Como otras imágenes en otros lugares —pero no tanto— las imágenes de Un Mundo Feliz no se imponen como obras, sino que inducen a una relación, un viaje y un compartir. El 68 no está muerto. Nada ha terminado, todavía queda algo. Y demos gracias, porque lo necesitaremos más que nunca para revertir el desorden de este mundo y evitar el regreso a lo anormal. ¡Por favor, sírvase!

SIGNS ARE THE LANGUAGE OF THE EYES

LES SIGNES SONT LE LANGAGE DES YEUX

LOS SIGNOS SON LA LENGUA DE LOS OJOS

FONS HICKMANN
—
BERLIN
MAY 9, 2020

Fons Hickmann
*studied design, photography, and philosophy and is
founder of the design studio 'Fons Hickmann M23'
in Berlin. He has taught at several universities, held
lectures and workshops around the world, and is
a professor at Berlin University of the Arts.
He is a member of TDC New York, Alliance Graphique
International, and Borussia Dortmund. Since 2018,
he has been the president of the association '100 Beste
Plakate' ('100 Best Posters' of Austria, Germany,
and Switzerland). He has published a few books
about design and football. Currently he lives with
his kids and a kitten in Berlin*
—
*il a étudié le graphisme, la photographie et la
philosophie et est le fondateur du studio de graphisme
"Fons Hickmann M23" à Berlin. Il a enseigné dans
plusieurs universités, a tenu des conférences et des
ateliers dans le monde entier et est professeur à
l'Université des Arts de Berlin. Il est membre du Type
Directors Club New York, de l'Alliance Graphique
International et du Borussia Dortmund. Depuis 2018,
il est le président de l'association "100 Beste Plakate"
(« Les 100 Meilleures Affiches » d'Autriche, d'Allemagne
et de Suisse). Il a publié quelques livres sur le design
et le football. Il vit actuellement à Berlin avec ses
enfants et son chat*
—
*estudió Diseño, Fotografía y Filosofía y es fundador
del estudio de diseño Fons Hickmann M23 en
Berlín. Ha enseñado en varias universidades, ha
dado conferencias y talleres en todo el mundo y es
profesor en la Universidad de las Artes de Berlín. Es
miembro de la TDC de Nueva York, de la AGI Alliance
Graphique International y de Borussia Dortmund.
Desde 2018 es el presidente de la asociación «100 Beste
Plakate» (100 Mejores Carteles de Austria, Alemania,
Suiza). Ha publicado varios libros sobre diseño y fútbol.
Actualmente vive con sus hijos y un gatito en Berlín*

*Sign o' the Times
Hurry before
it's too late
—Prince*

Every time has its signs, every sign has its meaning, and every meaning has its necessity.

When Sonia Diaz and Gabriel Martínez sent me the first layout of their book with the request for an accompanying word, I was struck by the diversity and inventiveness of their graphics. With a few strokes, dots, and shapes, the two designers create signs, symbols, and pictograms that possess explosive power.

The symbol has a long tradition in the history of political endorsement. As long as the struggle for human rights, political goals, and social purposes has been going on, artists and designers have been taking part in it. Without the signs that make an idea clear, without a symbol that unites a group of people, political agitation is hardly conceivable.

Humans need signs to orientate ourselves and protest needs signs to articulate itself. Sonia and Gabriel invent these signs with a seemingly inexhaustible abundance of ideas and a desire to provoke.

Aristotle defined the sign as something previously recognized that leads to the recognition of another. This book has a similar logic: I recognize something and form it into a sign, you understand the sign and carry it onward. This book is not a collection of artworks frozen in time, but a work in progress. It is not a graveyard of ideas past, but a motor for new ideas to come. It is a source of graphics that we can carry into the world and which will inspire us to create more ourselves.

It is a powder keg in a positive sense, and I can't wait to share it with my students.

ENG

Chaque époque a ses signes, chaque signe a sa signification et chaque signification a sa nécessité.

Lorsque Sonia Diaz et Gabriel Martínez m'ont envoyé la première mise en page de leur livre en me demandant un mot d'accompagnement, j'ai été frappé par la diversité et l'inventivité de leur graphisme. En quelques traits, points et formes, les deux graphistes créent des signes, des symboles et des pictogrammes qui ont un pouvoir explosif.

Le symbole a une longue tradition dans l'histoire de l'engagement politique. Depuis que la lutte pour les droits de l'homme, les objectifs politiques et les fins sociales existent, les artistes et les graphistes y prennent part. Sans les signes qui rendent une idée claire, sans un symbole qui unit un groupe de personnes, l'agitation politique est difficilement concevable.

L'homme a besoin de signes pour s'orienter et la protestation a besoin de signes pour s'articuler. Sonia et Gabriel inventent ces signes avec une profusion d'idées, apparemment inépuisable, et le désir de provoquer.

Aristote a défini le signe comme un élément préalablement reconnu, menant à la reconnaissance d'un autre. Ce livre présente une logique similaire : je reconnais tel élément et je le transforme en signe ; vous comprenez ce signe et vous le diffusez. Cet ouvrage n'est pas une collection d'œuvres d'art figées dans le temps, mais un travail en cours. Il ne s'agit pas d'un cimetière d'idées périmées, mais d'un moteur pour de nouvelles idées à venir. C'est une source de signes graphiques que nous pouvons diffuser dans le monde et qui nous incite à créer davantage nous-mêmes.

C'est une poudrière dans le sens positif du terme et j'ai hâte de la partager avec mes étudiants.

Cada tiempo tiene sus signos, cada signo tiene su significado, cada significado tiene su necesidad.

Cuando Sonia Díaz y Gabriel Martínez me pidieron un prólogo al enviarme la primera maqueta de su libro, la diversidad y la riqueza de ideas de sus imágenes me sobrecogieron. Con pocos trazos, puntos y formas, los dos diseñadores crean signos, símbolos y pictogramas de fuerza explosiva.

El símbolo tiene una larga tradición en la agitación política. Desde que se lucha por derechos y objetivos políticos y sociales, los artistas y diseñadores participan en esta guerra. Sin los signos que ilustran una idea, sin un símbolo que una a un grupo de personas, la agitación política es apenas imaginable.

El ser humano necesita los signos para orientarse, y la protesta necesita signos para articularse. Sonia y Gabriel inventan esos signos con una riqueza casi inagotable de ideas y con ganas de provocar.

Aristóteles definía el signo como algo antes reconocido que lleva al conocimiento de algo más. En esta lógica trabaja también este libro. Reconozco algo, lo convierto en un signo, tú comprendes el signo y lo llevas a otro lugar. Este libro no es una colección estática de obras de arte, este libro es una obra en marcha. Este libro no es un cementerio de ideas, es un motor para ideas nuevas. Es una fuente de piezas gráficas que podemos llevar al mundo y que nos inspira a desarrollar las nuestras.

Es un barril de pólvora positivo y estoy impaciente por colocarlo en la mesa frente a mis estudiantes.

FR

ES

PACKED CULTURAL VIRUSES

DES VIRUS CULTURELS EMBALLÉS

VIRUS CULTURALES EMPAQUETADOS

LINCOLN CUSHING
—
BERKELEY
MAY 2, 2020

Lincoln Cushing
*is an archivist and author who documents,
catalogs, and disseminates oppositional
political culture of the late 20th century.
His books include* Revolucion! Cuban
Poster Art, Visions of Peace & Justice, *and*
Agitate! Educate! Organize! - American
Labor Posters. *His research and publishing
projects can be seen at Docs Populi
(docspopuli.org)*

—

*archiviste et auteur, il documente,
inventorie et diffuse la culture d'opposition
politique de la fin du XXe siècle. Ses livres
comprennent* Revolucion! Cuban Poster
Art, Visions of Peace & Justice et Agitate!
Educate! Organize! - *American Labor
Posters. Ses projets de recherche et de
publication peuvent être consultés sur
Docs Populi (docspopuli.org)*

—

*es un archivista y autor que documenta,
cataloga y difunde la cultura política
de oposición de finales del siglo xx. Sus
libros incluyen* Revolucion! Cuban Poster
Art, Visions of Peace & Justice: Political
Posters *y* Agitate! Educate! Organize! -
American Labor Posters. *Sus proyectos
de investigación pueden verse en Docs
Populi (docspopuli.org)*

As Steven Heller notes, we are gripped in a global pandemic where everything is upside down. It is a useful analogy to see political graphics – framed here as 'pictomontages' – as densely packed cultural viruses. Freed of the limitations of language, they can rapidly transmit such abstract concepts as 'solidarity', 'sisterhood', or 'peace' all over the world.

Clean and modern pictomontages echo the very earliest forms of visual communication. Red ochre pigment stencils of human hands in the deep recesses of caves are at least 40,000 years old. But these were not public art, not as we know it. Our world is saturated with competing sensory stimulation, and activists for social change rely on graphic artists to develop visual viruses to persuade and mobilize the public.

This book calls out Rini Templeton (1935– 1986), whose work offers powerful lessons. One such lesson is that authenticity matters. Rini was deeply involved in the communities she represented; she drew people she knew and illustrated struggles she was part of. Another lesson: keep it simple. Her graphics were spare, black-and-white snapshots of the movement – images possible for an amateur to copy by hand onto a placard or paste into a layout for a printed flyer, in a world before desktop publishing and the Internet. Similar examples of dynamic, 'simple' graphics exploded in Paris during the 1968 general strike and in the United States in 1970, when the Vietnam war escalated and after students were shot and killed. The world was in turmoil and artistry played a role in making sense of it all. Then, screen printed images played an essential role in defining those movements. We need that now, before we are once again making red ochre stencils of our hands in caves.

Comme le note Steven Heller, nous sommes pris dans une pandémie mondiale où tout est sens dessus dessous. Voir des images politiques – présentées ici en tant que « pictomontages » - ressemblant à des virus culturels compactés, est une analogie tout à fait pertinente. Libérées des limites du langage, ces images peuvent rapidement transmettre des concepts abstraits, tels que la « solidarité », la « fraternité » ou la « paix » partout dans le monde.

Les pictomontages épurés et modernes font écho aux toutes premières formes de communication visuelle. Les empreintes ocre rouge de mains tracées au pochoir dans le fond des grottes datent d'au moins 40 000 ans. Mais ce n'était pas de l'art public, pas tel que nous l'entendons. Notre monde est saturé de stimulations sensorielles contradictoires et les militants qui luttent pour le changement social ont recours aux artistes pour développer des virus visuels, afin de persuader le public et de le mobiliser.

Ce livre invoque Rini Templeton (1935-1986), dont l'œuvre est riche en enseignements. L'authenticité compte, voilà l'un de ces enseignements. Rini était profondément impliquée dans les communautés qu'elle représentait ; elle dessinait les personnes qu'elle connaissait et illustrait les luttes auxquelles elle prenait part. Un autre encore : faire simple. Ses dessins étaient des sobres instantanés de mouvement en noir et blanc des images qu'un amateur pouvait copier à la main sur une affiche ou coller dans une mise en page pour un réaliser un flyer imprimé, et ce, dans un monde qui ne connaissait pas encore la publication assistée par ordinateur et Internet. Des exemples similaires de graphisme dynamique et « simple » ont explosé à Paris pendant la grève générale de 68 et aux États-Unis en 1970, lorsque la guerre du Vietnam s'est intensifiée et après le massacre d'étudiants, tués par balle. Le monde était en plein bouleversement et l'art a permis de donner un sens à tout cela. Ensuite, les images sérigraphiées ont joué un rôle essentiel dans la définition de ces mouvements. Nous avons besoin de cela maintenant, avant de refaire des pochoirs ocre rouge de nos mains dans les grottes.

Como señala Steven Heller, estamos atrapados en una pandemia global donde todo está al revés. Es una analogía útil para ver los gráficos políticos —enmarcados aquí como *pictomontajes*— como virus culturales densamente empaquetados. Libres de las limitaciones del lenguaje, pueden transmitir rápidamente conceptos abstractos como *solidaridad, hermandad o paz* en todo el mundo.

Los pictomontajes limpios y modernos se hacen eco de las primeras formas de comunicación visual. Las plantillas de pigmentos de ocre rojo de las manos humanas en los profundos recovecos de las cuevas tienen al menos 40.000 años. Pero no eran arte público tal como lo conocemos. Nuestro mundo está saturado de estímulos sensoriales que compiten entre sí, y los activistas por el cambio social confían en los artistas gráficos para desarrollar virus visuales que persuadan y movilicen al público.

Este libro evoca a Rini Templeton (1935-1986), cuyo trabajo ofrece poderosas lecciones. Una de ellas es que *la autenticidad importa*. Rini estaba profundamente involucrada en las comunidades que representaba; dibujaba a las personas que conocía e ilustraba las luchas de las que formaba parte. Otra es: *mantenlo simple*. Sus gráficos eran instantáneas en blanco y negro del movimiento, imágenes que un aficionado puede copiar a mano en una pancarta o pegar en un diseño para un folleto impreso en un mundo anterior a la autoedición y a internet. Ejemplos similares de gráficos dinámicos y *sencillos* explotaron en París durante la huelga general de 1968 y en los Estados Unidos en 1970 cuando se intensificó la guerra de Vietnam y después de que hubiera estudiantes muertos a tiros. El mundo estaba agitado y el arte desempeñaba un papel importante para buscar el sentido de aquello. Por entonces, las imágenes serigrafiadas tuvieron un papel esencial en la definición de esos movimientos. Eso mismo necesitamos ahora, antes de que acabemos estampando de nuevo plantillas de ocre rojo de nuestras manos en las cuevas.

NOBODY REALLY DOESN'T KNOW ANYTHING

PERSONNE NE SAIT RIEN

EN REALIDAD NADIE SABE NADA

KING ADZ
—
APRIL 19, 2020

King ADZ
*is on the front line of creative culture.
He is a chief creative officer, writer,
and film-maker, constantly pursuing
the leading edge of the zeitgeist*
—
*il est est en première ligne de la
culture créative. Il est directeur
artistique, écrivain et photographe,
toujours dans l'air du temps*
—
*está en primera línea de la cultura
creativa. Es un director creativo,
escritor y cineasta que está
constantemente persiguiendo la
vanguardia del espíritu de la época*

I have always been an outcast, from my conception (a tussle in a tent in 1968), the moment and circumstances of my birth (Lewisham General 1969), all through my upbringing and professional life, to sat here typing this right now, I've been on the outside looking in. And this is my superpower to quote Ye. And talking of power, I've been talking about how content (the outcast) always champions over advertising (the mainstream) for a decade now, and thankfully content is a force that's about to come into it's own.

As weird and as completely fucked as this may sound in a book about creative protest and activism, the only way to make any real kind of change is to vote with your pound dollar euro shekel rand rupee, as brands hold all the power and money. Your vote is worthless (the old joke goes 'don't vote because a politician will get in' has never been so relevant) as democracy has become a cruel slight of hand currently demonstrated by that fuckwit triumvirate of Donald Trump, Boris Johnson, and Jair Bolsonaro. If these men represent the mainstream then I'm proud to be an outcast for life. And as I'm on the outside looking in, this where I start to think and create differently, and the one true culture that has the biggest influence on me is street culture.

Street culture is the wallpaper for Generation X, Y, Z and Alpha. It's also the soundtrack, menu, style bible and most definitely the flavour of content. Content was born out of street culture. Content and street culture are two sides to the same coin. Just as street art (the outsider) blew up the art world (the mainstream), content (outsider) did the same to the traditional worlds of media, advertising, marketing and PR. And if you want your audience to respond to it (rather than ignore) your content has to look like you know what your doing and this can only be achieved through capturing the look and feel of street culture and serving it up in the first few seconds of your piece of content. This is why a lot of brands/agencies/politicians get it so wrong. This is why they will never really make any content that people actually relate to. Make it reflect the culture, and right now the number one major force in our current culture is doing good — which basically boils down to being honest, upfront, and nice to people, the planet, animals, and respecting all kinds of beliefs, flavours, and walks of life. It doesn't get much simpler than

this. If your brand mission doesn't tick those boxes then you're fucked. You'll get found out.

Doing good as a brand means that people are buying into you because of what you stand for, not what you cost. In the old days it was Buy One Get One Free now it's freedom through choice, and this choice is dictated by an inner voice telling you that a certain brand is doing good and so its okay to take it off the shelf and consume. That the end result is a positive one for everyone — as it as there will be a hidden benefit, not a hidden cost. Thanks to the airwaves being democratised, you now know which brand is doing what to help, and which aren't doing anything at all. A bit like when Coke refused to stop producing single-use plastic.

But to get to that point you would have needed to have consumed some content that alerts you to some proof that the brand is doing some good somewhere; making a real difference. But these messages have to break through the black hole of content that currently clogs the digital airwaves up. And this black hole is no freak accident. It's there to ensure you pay the toll; pay for that algorithm that ensures that your ideas and content is getting out there. In the old days something could go viral (*The Evolution of Dance; Kony 2012; naked Kim; Charlie Bit My Finger; JK wedding entry dance; Keyboard Cat*) but now that doesn't happen as Google owns the world and you have to pay them to play in it.

Love your culture. Make original content. Pay the algorithm toll. Spread the word. Change the world.

Only brands can afford to do this properly, but saying that I recently created some great work for a brand whose head of content really didn't know anything about the subject, proving that nobody really doesn't know anything.

ENG

J'ai toujours été un paria depuis ma conception (une bagarre dans une tente en 1968), le moment et les circonstances de ma naissance (Lewisham General 1969), au cours de mon éducation et de ma vie professionnelle et en ce moment même, en écrivant ces mots. Je reste à l'extérieur à regarder ce qui se passe à l'intérieur. Et c'est mon super pouvoir, pour citer Ye. En parlant de pouvoir, je dis depuis dix ans que le contenu (le marginal) l'emporte toujours sur la publicité (le courant dominant) et, heureusement, le contenu est une force qui est sur le point de s'imposer.

Ce que je dis, aussi bizarre et complètement foireux que cela puisse paraître, dans un livre sur la contestation et l'activisme créatifs, c'est que la seule manière de réaliser un vrai changement, c'est de voter avec votre livre sterling-dollar-euro-shekel-rand-roupie, vu que les marques détiennent tout le pouvoir et l'argent. Votre vote ne vaut rien (la vieille blague « Ne votez pas parce qu'un politicien sera élu » n'a jamais été aussi juste), car la démocratie est devenue un cruel tour de passe-passe, comme en témoigne aujourd'hui ce triumvirat de crétins, composé de Donald Trump, Boris Johnson et Jair Bolsonaro. Si ces types représentent le courant dominant, alors je suis fier d'être un marginal à vie. Et comme je suis à l'extérieur à regarder à l'intérieur, c'est là que je commence à penser et à créer différemment et c'est la culture de la rue, la seule vraie culture qui a la plus grande influence sur moi.

La *street culture* est le fond d'écran des générations X, Y, Z et Alpha. C'est aussi la bande-son, le menu, la bible du style et, bien sûr, la saveur du contenu. Le contenu est issu de la *street culture*. Le contenu et la *street culture* sont les deux faces d'une même pièce. Tout comme le *street art* (l'outsider) a fait exploser le monde de l'art (le courant dominant), le contenu (l'outsider) a fait de même avec le monde traditionnel des médias, de la publicité, du marketing et des relations publiques. Et si tu veux que ton public réagisse à ton contenu (plutôt que de l'ignorer), il doit donner l'impression que tu sais ce que tu fais. Cela n'est possible qu'en capturant le *look and feel* de la *street culture* et en les diffusant dès les premières secondes de ton contenu. C'est la raison pour laquelle beaucoup de marques, d'agences et de politiciens se trompent autant. Voilà pourquoi ils ne créeront jamais réellement un contenu auquel les gens s'identifient. Faire en sorte qu'il reflète la culture et, en ce moment, la principale force de notre culture actuelle, c'est de faire le bien – ce qui se résume fondamentalement à être honnêtes, francs et gentils avec les gens, la planète et les animaux, et à respecter toutes sortes de croyances, de goûts et de modes de vie. Il n'y a pas plus simple que cela. Si la mission de ta marque ne coche pas toutes ces cases, alors tu es foutu. Tu vas te faire prendre.

Faire le bien en tant que marque signifie que les gens achètent tes produits pour ce que tu représentes et pas pour ce qu'ils coûtent. Avant, c'était « Deux au prix d'un », maintenant, c'est la liberté de choisir et ce choix est dicté par une voix intérieure qui te dit qu'une marque donnée agit bien et qu'il est donc normal d'acheter ses produits et de les consommer. Le résultat final est positif pour tout le monde, car il y aura un avantage caché et pas un coût caché. Grâce à la démocratisation des ondes, on sait maintenant quelle marque fait quelque chose de positif et celle qui ne fait rien du tout. Un peu comme lorsque Coke a refusé d'arrêter de produire du plastique à usage unique.

Mais pour en arriver là, il aurait fallu consommer un contenu qui t'avertisse et te prouve que cette marque agit bien quelque part, qu'elle change vraiment les choses. Pour cela, ces messages doivent percer le trou noir du contenu qui engorge actuellement les ondes numériques. Et ce trou noir n'est pas là par hasard, il est là pour que tu payes le prix fort, pour que tu casques pour cet algorithme qui garantit que tes idées et ton contenu soient diffusés. Avant, quelque chose pouvait devenir viral (The Evolution of Dance ; Kony 2012 ; naked Kim ; Charlie Bit My Finger ; JK wedding Entrance dance ; Keyboard Cat), mais aujourd'hui, cela n'arrive plus, car Google est le maître du monde et tu dois payer pour être diffusé.

Aime ta culture. Fais des contenus originaux. Paie le prix de l'algorithme. Fais passer le mot. Change le monde !

Seules les marques peuvent se permettre de bien faire les choses, mais ceci dit, j'ai récemment réalisé un beau boulot pour une marque dont le responsable du contenu ne savait vraiment rien sur la question, c'est bien la preuve que personne ne sait vraiment rien.

FR

Siempre he sido un marginado, desde mi concepción (un forcejeo en una tienda de campaña en 1968) y el momento y las circunstancias de mi nacimiento (Lewisham General, 1969), a lo largo de mi educación y vida profesional, hasta ahora mismo, sentado aquí para escribir esto, he estado fuera mirando hacia adentro. Y este es mi superpoder, por citar a Ye. Y hablando de poder, desde hace una década vengo diciendo que el contenido (el marginado) siempre se sobrepone a la publicidad (la corriente principal), y afortunadamente el contenido es una fuerza que está a punto de entrar en acción.

Por extraño y jodido que esto pueda sonar en un libro sobre la protesta creativa y el activismo, la única manera de hacer cualquier tipo de cambio real es votar con tu libra dólar euro shéquel rand rupia, ya que las marcas tienen todo el poder y el dinero. Tu voto no vale nada (el viejo chiste de «no votes porque un político se meterá» nunca había sido tan relevante) ya que la democracia se ha convertido en un cruel desaire que actualmente demuestra el triunvirato de gilipollas compuesto por Donald Trump, Boris Johnson y Jair Bolsonaro. Si estos hombres representan a la corriente principal, entonces estoy orgulloso de ser un paria de por vida. Y como estoy ahí afuera mirando hacia adentro, ahí es donde empiezo a pensar y crear de manera diferente, y la única cultura verdadera que tiene influencia en mí es la cultura de la calle.

La cultura de la calle es el fondo de pantalla de la Generación X, Y, Z y Alfa. También es la banda sonora, el menú, la biblia de estilo y, definitivamente, el sabor del contenido. El contenido nació de la cultura callejera. El contenido y la cultura callejera son dos caras de la misma moneda. Así como el arte callejero (el forastero) hizo explotar el mundo del arte (la corriente principal), el contenido (el marginal) hizo lo mismo con los mundos tradicionales de los medios, la publicidad, el marketing y las relaciones públicas. Y si quieres que tu audiencia responda a ello (en lugar de ignorarlo) tu contenido tiene que hacer ver que sabes lo que estás haciendo, y esto sólo se puede lograr capturando el aspecto y las sensaciones de la cultura callejera y sirviéndolo en los primeros segundos de tu pieza de contenido. Por esta razón, muchas marcas / agencias / políticos se equivocan. Es por eso que nunca harán ningún contenido con el que la gente se identifique realmente.

Haced que refleje la cultura, y en este momento la fuerza principal de nuestra cultura es hacer el bien, lo que básicamente se reduce a ser honesto, directo y amable con la gente, el planeta, los animales, y respetar todo tipo de creencias, sabores y estilos de vida. No hay nada más simple que esto. Si la misión de tu marca no cumple con esos requisitos, estás jodido. Te descubrirán.

Hacer el bien como marca significa que la gente te compra por lo que representas, no por lo que cuestas. En los viejos tiempos era «compre uno y llévese otro gratis», ahora es la libertad a través de la elección, y esta elección está dictada por una voz interior que te dice que una cierta marca está haciendo el bien y que está bien que la tomes del estante y la consumas. Que el resultado final es positivo para todos, ya que habrá un beneficio oculto, no un costo oculto. Gracias a la democratización de las ondas aéreas, ahora sabes qué marca está haciendo lo que debe para mejorar, y cuáles no están haciendo nada en absoluto. Un poco como cuando Coca-Cola se negó a dejar de producir plástico de un solo uso.

Para llegar a ese punto, tienes que haber consumido algún contenido que te dé alguna prueba de que la marca está haciendo algo bueno en algún lugar, marcando una verdadera diferencia, pero tales mensajes tienen que romper el agujero negro de contenido que actualmente obstruye las ondas digitales. Y este agujero negro no es un extraño accidente. Está ahí para asegurarse de que pagues el peaje; paga por ese algoritmo que asegura que tus ideas y tu contenido salgan a la luz. En los viejos tiempos algo podía volverse viral (*La evolución del baile; Kony 2012; Kim desnuda; Charlie me mordió el dedo; JK Wedding Entrance Dance; Keyboard Cat*), pero ahora eso no sucede, ya que Google es dueño del mundo y tienes que pagarles para poder entrar en el juego.

Ama tu cultura. Haz contenido original. Paga el peaje del algoritmo. Corre la voz. Cambia el mundo.

Sólo las marcas pueden permitirse hacer esto correctamente, pero si os digo que hace poco realicé un gran trabajo para una marca cuyo jefe de contenido prácticamente no sabía nada sobre el tema, eso demuestra que en realidad nadie sabe nada.

AN AIM
AN ENIGMA

UN OBJECTIF
UNE ÉNIGME

UNA FINALIDAD
UN ENIGMA

JORDI CLARAMONTE
—
MADRID
APRIL 29, 2020

I consider the central object of aesthetics to be the living and mutating set of 'ways of doing', the modes of relationship through which languages, subjects, and communities self-organize. To that end, of course, aesthetics is radically linked to the ethical and political. But it establishes this connection without agreeing to merge with these spheres and their respective reasons. And this is not because of any ivory tower imperative, but because the estrangement of the aesthetic – its enigmatic nature and even a certain tactical frivolity that it usually displays – is among the few guarantees that we can count on to avoid becoming preachers of this or that morality.

One of the silliest and most recalcitrant bits of nonsense that haunts us is that which leads people – who are, by the way, very intelligent – to consider that for artistic production to have political effectiveness, it is essential for it to renounce any hint of complexity, contradiction, or vividness of any kind. Which obviously stinks, bringing to mind a monstrous hybrid combining Botín's[1] mug with Stalin's moustache.

The fact is that nothing in our classical culture forces us to bury ourselves with such creatures. In Greek, 'telos' means purpose, but lo and behold, when they passed that word into the plural ('tele'), it no longer meant 'purposes', but rather 'mystery'. When a thing has an end, then it has an end and that's that. But when it has several ends, then what it has is an enigma. An enigma that in no way diminishes the political power of the work, but instead reinforces it, because it makes it composite, polyhedral – like a diamond or the eye of a butterfly.

Jordi Claramonte
studied philosophy at UNED and electricity at a vocational school. Like many of the 'insubordinates' in the military service, he was sentenced to 14 years of disenfranchisement, thanks to which he had time to think and do things in collectives such as La Fiambrera Obrera, SCCPP.org, and YoMango. He works as a professor of aesthetics at UNED and writes books on porn, militarism, autonomy, context art, and modal aesthetics
—
il a étudié la philosophie à l'UNED et l'électricité dans une école professionnelle. Comme beaucoup d' « insubordonnés » au cours de leur service militaire, il a été privé du droit électoral pendant 14 ans, période pendant laquelle il a eu le temps de réfléchir et de s'engager dans des collectifs comme La Fiambrera Obrera, SCCPP.org et YoMango. Il travaille comme professeur d'esthétique à l'UNED et écrit des livres sur le porno, le militarisme, l'autonomie, l'art contextuel et l'esthétique modale
—
estudió Filosofía en la UNED y electricidad. Como a muchos de los insumisos al servicio militar le cayó una condena de 14 años de inhabilitación, gracias a lo cual tuvo tiempo para pensar y hacer cosas en colectivos como La Fiambrera Obrera, SCCPP.org o YoMango. Trabaja como Profesor de Estética en la UNED y escribe libros sobre porno, militarismo, autonomía, arte de contexto y Estética Modal

1 *Emilio Botín* (1934-2014) was an aggressive Spanish banker, president of Banco Santander between 1986 and 2014

ENG

Je considère que l'objet central de l'esthétique est l'ensemble vivant et en mutation des « façons de faire », les modes de relation par lesquels les langues, les sujets et les communautés s'auto-organisent. À cette fin, bien sûr, l'esthétique est radicalement liée à l'éthique et au politique. Mais elle établit ce lien sans accepter de fusionner avec ces sphères et leurs différents motifs. Et ce, non pas en raison d'un quelconque impératif de couper les ponts et de s'isoler, mais parce que l'aliénation de l'esthétique - son caractère énigmatique et, je dirais même, la frivolité tactique dont elle fait montre habituellement - est l'une des rares garanties sur lesquelles nous pouvons compter pour éviter de devenir des prêcheurs de telle ou telle morale.

Une des énormités les plus absurdes et les plus coriaces qui nous poursuit est celle qui pousse les gens - qui sont d'ailleurs très intelligents - à considérer que, pour que la production artistique ait une efficacité politique, il faut absolument qu'elle renonce à toute trace de complexité, à toute pointe de contradiction ou d'acuité de quelque nature que ce soit. Ce qui est évidemment douteux, si l'on pense à un hybride monstrueux, qui combine la tronche de Botín[1] à la moustache de Staline.

Rien dans notre culture classique ne nous oblige à nous enterrer avec de telles créatures. En grec, le terme « telos » signifie « but », mais - oh surprise ! - une fois au pluriel (« tele »), il ne veut plus dire « but », mais plutôt « mystère ». Lorsqu'une chose a une fin, alors elle a une fin, point final. Mais quand elle a plusieurs fins, alors c'est qu'elle est une énigme. Une énigme qui ne diminue en rien le pouvoir politique de l'œuvre, mais au contraire le renforce, car elle la rend composite, polyédrique - comme un diamant ou l'œil d'un papillon.

Considero que el objeto central de la Estética es el conjunto vivo y mutante de «modos de hacer», de los *modos de relación* mediante los que lenguajes, sujetos y comunidades se autoorganizan. En esa medida —claro está— la Estética se vincula radicalmente con lo ético y lo político. Pero lo hace sin acceder a fundirse con dichos ámbitos y sus respectivas razones. Y eso no por ningún imperativo torremarfilesco sino porque el extrañamiento de lo estético, su enigma e incluso cierta frivolidad táctica de la que suele hacer gala, son una de las pocas garantías con que podemos contar para no convertirnos en predicadores de esta o aquella moral.

Una de las tonterías más tontas y más recalcitrantes que nos acecha es la que lleva a gente —por otra parte muy inteligente— a considerar que para que la producción artística pueda tener una cierta efectividad política es imprescindible que renuncie a cualquier atisbo de complejidad, contradicción o vidilla de cualquier tipo. Y claro, eso apesta y nos hace pensar en un monstruoso híbrido que uniera la jeta de Botín[1] con el bigote de Stalin.

El caso es que nada en nuestra cultura clásica nos obliga a achantar con semejantes criaturas. En griego *telos* significa «finalidad», pero hete aquí que cuando pasaban esa palabra al plural, que era *tele*, ya no significaba «finalidades», sino «misterio». Cuando una cosa tiene un fin, pues tiene un fin y santaspascuas. Ahora bien cuando tiene varios fines, entonces lo que tiene es un enigma. Un enigma que no mengua en absoluto la potencia política de la obra, antes bien la refuerza porque la hace compuesta, poliédrica como un diamante o el ojo de una mariposa.

---

1 *Emilio Botín (1934-2014) était un banquier espagnol ambitieux, le président du groupe bancaire Santander entre 1986 et 2014*

1 *Emilio Botín (1934-2014), también llamado* el banquero agresivo, *fue presidente del Banco Santander entre 1986 y 2014*

PR⚀TEST DES⚀GN

DESIGN DE LA C⚀NTESTATI⚀N

D⚀SEÑ⚀ DE PR⚀TESTA

TOM BIELING

—

HAMBURG
JULY 15, 2020

Over the last decades, the number, diversity, and vigour of social movements has increased, and the world has witnessed the global rise of a relatively new kind of activism, in which political protest often makes use of designedly tools, creative methods, and artistic expressions. We find some popular examples in the distinctive images of resistance – posters, graphics, stickers, t-shirts, memes, street art, paintings, performances and video clips – that hold a prominent place in the world's visual heritage. Here, the line is often thin between underground and pop cultures.

The corresponding tactics and strategies are found in the fields of visual communication and material cultures. They are meant to stimulate discourse and action, and to help marginalized, underprivileged communities to express themselves, communicate with a wider public, and sustain networks in- and outside of social movements.

On a technical, functional level, this form of design activism is often embedded in virtual or material artefacts or media. On a rhetorical level, it is often combined with humour, satire, subversion, provocation, and irony, in an attempt to develop counter-narratives, to demonstrate alternative proposals for the future, and to furthermore provide impetus for their implementation.

Drawing attention to a topic is obviously only one step, albeit an important one, for mobilizing the public and changing its perceptions and behaviour. Design is involved not only in this step, however, but also in all further steps. On a communicative level, design takes on a double function here: by questioning existing orders and hierarchies, it makes change conceivable in the first place. Design can therefore create visions of a better future and at the same time, through its practical actions, itself establish them. By absorbing and reassembling a broad range of symbolisms, signs, and imagery, it creates not only new aesthetics but also new meanings, and thus reveals itself to both designers and recipients as a means of challenging and critically questioning dominant power systems.

Dr. Tom Bieling
author of Design (&) Activism
*(2019) and other publications on
the political dimensions of design*

—

auteur de Design (&) Activism
*(2019) et d'autres publications sur
les dimensions politiques du design*

—

autor de Design (&) Activism
*(2019) y otras publicaciones sobre
las dimensiones políticas del diseño*

ENG

Au cours des dernières décennies, le nombre, la diversité et la vigueur des mouvements sociaux se sont accrus et le monde a assisté à la montée globale d'un type d'activisme relativement nouveau, dans lequel la protestation politique fait souvent appel à des outils, des méthodes créatives et des expressions artistiques conçus à dessein. Nous en trouvons quelques exemples populaires dans les images caractéristiques de la résistance - affiches, graphiques, autocollants, t-shirts, mèmes, street art, peintures, performances et clips vidéo - qui occupent une place prépondérante dans le patrimoine visuel mondial. Ici, la frontière est souvent mince entre les cultures underground et pop.

Les tactiques et stratégies correspondantes se trouvent dans les domaines de la communication visuelle et des cultures matérielles. Elles visent à stimuler le discours et l'action, et à aider les communautés marginalisées et défavorisées à s'exprimer, à communiquer avec un public plus large et à entretenir des réseaux à l'intérieur et à l'extérieur des mouvements sociaux.

Sur le plan technique et fonctionnel, cette forme d'activisme est souvent intégrée dans des artefacts ou des médias virtuels et matériels. Sur le plan rhétorique, elle est souvent associée à l'humour, à la satire, à la subversion, à la provocation et à l'ironie, pour tenter de développer une contre-propagande, de présenter des propositions alternatives pour l'avenir et, en outre, de donner une impulsion à leur mise en œuvre.

Attirer l'attention sur un sujet n'est évidemment qu'une étape, certes importante, pour mobiliser le public et changer ses perceptions et son comportement. La conception est toutefois impliquée non seulement dans cette étape, mais aussi dans toutes les étapes suivantes. Sur le plan de la communication, le design remplit ici une double fonction : en remettant en question les hiérarchies et les ordres existants, il rend le changement concevable au départ. Le design peut dès lors créer des visions d'un avenir meilleur et, en même temps, par ses actions pratiques, les mettre en place lui-même. En absorbant et en rassemblant un large éventail de symbolismes, de signes et d'images, il génère non seulement de nouvelles esthétiques mais aussi de nouvelles significations et se révèle ainsi aux designers et aux destinataires comme un moyen de remettre en question et de critiquer les systèmes de pouvoir dominants.

En las últimas décadas el número, la diversidad y el vigor de los movimientos sociales han crecido, y el mundo ha contemplado el advenimiento global de un tipo de activismo relativamente novedoso, en el que con frecuencia la protesta política hace uso de herramientas específicas, métodos creativos y expresiones artísticas. Encontramos ejemplos conocidos de ello en esas imágenes de resistencia distintivas —pósteres, grafismo, pegatinas, camisetas, memes, arte de la calle, pinturas, performances y clips de vídeo— que tienen un lugar destacado en el patrimonio visual del mundo. Aquí, la línea entre las culturas underground y pop suele ser delgada.

En los campos de la comunicación visual y la cultura material, encontramos tácticas y estrategias análogas destinadas a estimular el discurso y la acción y ayudar a las comunidades marginadas y desfavorecidas a expresarse a sí mismas, comunicarse con un público más amplio y mantener redes sociales dentro y fuera de los movimientos sociales.

En el aspecto técnico y funcional, esta forma de activismo del diseño se presenta a menudo integrada en obras de arte o en medios virtuales o materiales. En el aspecto retórico, suele combinarse con humor, sátira, subversión, provocación e ironía, con la intención de desarrollar contranarrativas, demostrar propuestas alternativas para el futuro y, además, proporcionar impulsos para su implementación.

Llamar la atención sobre un tema es obviamente sólo un paso, aunque importante, para movilizar al público y cambiar sus percepciones y sus conductas. El diseño participa no sólo en este paso, sino en todos los siguientes. En el aspecto comunicativo, el diseño tiene aquí una doble función: ante todo, al cuestionar el orden y las jerarquías establecidos hace que el cambio sea concebible. A partir de ahí, el diseño crea visiones de un futuro mejor y, al mismo tiempo, las establece con sus acciones. Al absorber y reensamblar una amplia gama de simbolismos, signos e imaginerías, no sólo crea estéticas nuevas sino también nuevos significados, y se revela así, para los diseñadores y para el público, como una manera de desafiar y cuestionar de manera crítica los sistemas de poder dominantes.

M☠RE THAN A SPASM

PLUS QU'UN SPASME

MÁS QUE UN ESPASM☠

NATALIA MIRAPEIX BEDIA
& VOCES CON FUTURA
—
MADRID
APRIL 20, 2020

Natalia Mirapeix Bedia
*is a multidisciplinary creative who
works with meaningful and exciting
ideas, strategies, and images. She has
an undergraduate degree in advertising
and public relations, a master's degree
in art direction, and a postgraduate
degree in illustration and comics*
—
*c'est une créatrice multidisciplinaire
qui travaille avec des idées, des
stratégies et des images significatives
et passionnantes. Elle est titulaire d'un
diplôme de premier cycle en publicité
et relations publiques, d'une maîtrise
en direction artistique et d'un diplôme
de troisième cycle en illustration
et bande dessinée*
—
*es una creativa multidisciplinar que
trabaja con ideas, estrategias e imágenes
significativas y emocionantes. Y está
licenciada en Publicidad y Relaciones
Públicas, es Máster en Dirección de Arte
y Posgraduada en Ilustración y Cómic*

When the #15m movement exploded in 2011 and I created vocesconfutura.org, I didn't have much in the way of contemporary references for graphic activism. Although I had been an activist in the student union, the truth is that I only had some basic knowledge on graphic design and protest, acquired in obligatory art history lessons in high school or university. Plus a little here and a little there from some reading on the Internet.

I think the first of Sonia and Gabriel Freeman's posters reached its platform not far from the second week of the 'Quincemayista' movement. Since that time, I have actively participated in all the graphic outpourings that have taken place in this country, and in each of them, Un Mundo Feliz has appeared. Moreover, during this time, they have allowed me to get closer to their way of thinking and practicing design.

I think that, within the guild – as Raquel Pelta once pointed out to me – there are many designers who do 'occasional activism' to shake off the monotony and hypocrisy of the labour market that buries them. But activist designers? There are very few.

I've been away from the flow of visible graphic protest for a few months, because both its artificial implementation in the institutional sphere and its excessively virtual character have worn me out. Un Mundo Feliz is more than a spasm or a creative exercise with superfluously identitarian intentions. I believe that Sonia and Gabriel are the reference that I did not have and that I am happy now – and forever – to be able to have. Thanks for everything.

>>> Voces con Futura was born in May 2011 as a result of the citizen mobilization that has come to be known as 15-M. It is a freely downloadable image bank in which designers, illustrators, and activists make their banners and posters available to the public for social demonstration in support of the movements #15m, #spanishrevolution, #globalrevolution, #worldrevolution, #occupy, #99%, #democraciarealya, and #realdemocracynow. As Liz McQuiston wrote in her book, *Visual Impact: Creative Dissent in the 21st Century*, 'los indignados'/15M have left in this site a continuing visual legacy as well as Spain's largest protest poster exhibition.

ENG

Lorsque le mouvement #15m a explosé en 2011 et que j'ai créé vocesconfutura.org, je n'avais pas beaucoup de références contemporaines sur le militantisme graphique. Bien que j'aie été militante au sein du syndicat étudiant, sur le graphisme et la protestation, je n'avais en réalité que quelques connaissances de base, acquises lors des cours obligatoires d'histoire de l'art au lycée ou à l'université. Plus quelques informations glanées ici et là grâce à des lectures sur Internet.

Je pense que la première affiche de Sonia et Gabriel Freeman a été présentée sur sa plateforme aux alentours de la deuxième semaine du mouvement « Quincemayista ». Depuis lors, j'ai participé activement à toutes les manifestations graphiques qui ont eu lieu dans ce pays, et, à chacune d'elles, Un Mundo Feliz était présent. En outre, pendant toute cette période, ses membres m'ont permis de me rapprocher de leur façon de penser et de pratiquer le graphisme.

Je pense que, au sein de la « corporation » - comme Raquel Pelta me l'a fait remarquer un jour - il y a beaucoup de graphistes qui font du « militantisme occasionnel » pour sortir de l'ennui et se défaire de l'hypocrisie du marché du travail qui les engluent. Mais des graphistes militants ? Il y en a très peu.

Je me suis éloignée de l'afflux de protestations graphiques visibles pendant quelques mois, car tant son déploiement artificiel dans le domaine institutionnel que son caractère excessivement virtuel m'ont épuisée. Un Mundo Feliz est plus qu'un spasme ou qu'un exercice créatif avec des intentions identitaires superflues. Je crois que Sonia et Gabriel sont les références qui me manquaient et je suis heureuse maintenant - et je le serai toujours - de pouvoir les avoir. Merci pour tout.

Cuando en 2011 estalló el #15m y creé *vocesconfutura.org* no tenía demasiados referentes contemporáneos de activismo gráfico. Aunque había sido militante del Sindicato de Estudiantes lo cierto es que, si hablamos de diseño gráfico y protesta, sólo tenía unos conocimientos básicos adquiridos en las lecciones obligatorias de Historia del Arte en el instituto o la universidad. Un poco de aquí y otro poco de allá de alguna lectura por Internet.

Creo que el primer cartel de Sonia y Gabriel Freeman debió llegar a la plataforma no más tarde de la segunda semana del movimiento *quincemayista*. Desde entonces, he participado en todos los desbordes gráficos que ha habido en este país de manera activa y en todos ellos Un mundo feliz ha aparecido. A su manera, eso siempre. Además, durante este tiempo, me han permitido acercarme a su método de pensar y ejercer el diseño.

Creo que, dentro del gremio —como me apuntó Raquel Pelta por aquel entonces— hay muchos diseñadores que hacen «activismo eventual» por sacudirse la monotonía y la hipocresía del mercado laboral que les sepulta. ¿Diseñadores activistas? Pocos.

Yo llevo unos meses lejos del fluir de la protesta gráfica visible porque tanto su implementación artificiosa en lo institucional como su excesivo carácter virtual han acabado por cansarme. Un Mundo Feliz es algo más que un espasmo o ejercicio creativo con intenciones superfluamente identitarias. Creo que Sonia y Gabriel son el referente que no tuve y que me alegro ahora —y por siempre— de poder tener. Gracias por todo.

>>> *Voces con Futura* a vu le jour en mai 2011, suite à la mobilisation citoyenne connue sous le nom de 15-M. Il s'agit d'une banque d'images librement téléchargeables dans laquelle des graphistes, des illustrateurs et des militants mettent leurs bannières et leurs affiches à la disposition du public pour les manifestations sociales de soutien aux mouvements #15m, #spanishrevolution, #globalrevolution, #worldrevolution, #occupy, #99%, #democraciarealya et #realdemocracynow. Comme l'a écrit Liz McQuiston dans son livre, *Visual Impact : Creative Dissent in the 21st Century*, « los indignados »/15M ont laissé sur ce site un héritage visuel permanent et la plus grande exposition d'affiches de contestation d'Espagne.

>>> *Voces con Futura* nació en mayo de 2011, fruto de la movilización ciudadana que ha llegado a conocerse con el nombre de 15-M. Es un banco de imágenes de libre descarga en el que diseñadores, ilustradores y activistas ponen sus carteles reivindicativos a disposición de la ciudadanía para la movilización social y el apoyo de los movimientos #15m #spanishrevolution #globalrevolution #worldrevolution #ocuppy #99% #democraciarealya #realdemocracynow. Como escribe Liz McQuiston en su libro *Visual Impact. Creative Dissent in the 21st Century*, los indignados/15M dejaron en esta web un continuo legado visual y la mayor muestra de carteles de protesta de España.

FR

ES

THIS BOOK IS ONLY A STARTING POINT

CE LIVRE N'EST QU'UN POINT DE DÉPART

ESTE LIBRO ES SOLO UN PUNTO DE PARTIDA

STEVE LAMBERT
—
NEW YORK
MAY 17, 2020

Steve Lambert
*is the co-founder and co-director of the
Center for Artistic Activism, a research
and training institute helping activists be
more creative and artists be more effective.
Over the past five years, his focus has
been on collaborating with sex workers on
campaigns for human rights, fighting for
safe consumption places for drug users*

—

*il est le co-fondateur et le co-directeur
du Center for Artistic Activism, un institut
de recherche et de formation qui aide les
militants à développer leur créativité et les
artistes à améliorer leur efficacité. Depuis
cinq ans, il collabore activement avec les
travailleurs du sexe, dans le cadre des
campagnes pour les droits de l'homme,
et se bat pour l'ouverture d'espaces
pour les toxicomanes afin qu'ils puissent
consommer sans danger*

—

*es cofundador y codirector del Center
for Artistic Activism, un instituto de
investigación y formación que ayuda a los
activistas a ser más creativos y a los artistas
a ser más eficaces. En los últimos cinco
años se ha centrado en colaborar con los
trabajadores del sexo en campañas por
los derechos humanos, y con personas
que usan drogas en la lucha por espacios
de consumo seguros*

There are millions of ways to win a campaign. Well-made graphics may accelerate progress, though a creative strategy is critical. Too many get focused on tactics and aesthetics, but we know reflexively that rehashing stale methods – a march, an occupation, a boycott, a petition - becomes less effective each time they are repeated. So, we must come up with bold objectives and new ways to achieve them.

Once you've clarified what you hope to achieve, let the unusual combinations of imagery you see in these pages serve as inspiration. Mash together popular, well-known concepts with radical and unusual ideas. Wrap liberatory messages in comfortable packages. Take complex perspectives and fold them into simple forms.

This book shows some techniques and offers examples. You can borrow from them, recombine them with others you know, or cast them aside and develop your own. Remember, the examples are not the outcome. This book is only a starting point, and while it may feel good to have it in your collection, your role does not end in merely possessing it. You can continue what is started in these pages, and activate the ideas by combining them with your own.

Consider what you want people to think about. What do you want them to feel? And, most importantly, what do you want them *to do*? Then mix existing methods in new ways to move us closer to a world that is just and equitable, playful and fun, smarter and more compassionate.

* * *

*Art is a bridge
that connects
uncommon, idealistic,
or even radical ideas
with everyday life.
It's important
to be able to laugh
while actively
questioning
the various power
structures at work
in our daily lives*

* * *

ENG
....

Il existe des millions de façons de gagner une campagne. Des dessins bien faits peuvent accélérer davantage les progrès, mais avoir une stratégie créative reste essentiel. Trop nombreux encore sont ceux qui se concentrent sur la tactique et l'esthétique, mais on sait par réflexe que les vieilles méthodes - une marche, une occupation, un boycott, une pétition - perdent de leur efficacité à chaque fois qu'elles sont répétées. Aussi devons-nous trouver des objectifs audacieux et de nouveaux moyens de les atteindre.

Dès que vous savez exactement ce que vous voulez obtenir, laissez-vous inspirer par les combinaisons insolites d'images de ces pages. Amalgamez les fameux concepts populaires avec des idées radicales et inhabituelles. Emballez joliment vos messages libérateurs. Prenez des angles complexes, pliez-les et faites-en des formes simples.

Cet ouvrage présente des techniques et propose des exemples. Vous pouvez emprunter ces images, les recombiner avec d'autres que vous connaissez ou les laisser de côté et créer les vôtres. N'oubliez pas que ces modèles ne représentent pas l'aboutissement. Ce livre n'est qu'un point de départ et, même si l'ajouter à votre collection vous fait plaisir, votre rôle ne se limite pas à l'avoir dans votre bibliothèque. Vous pouvez poursuivre ce qui a été commencé dans ces pages et déclencher les idées en les combinant avec les vôtres.

Réfléchissez à ce que vous voulez que les gens pensent. Que voulez-vous qu'ils ressentent ? Et, surtout, que voulez-vous *qu'ils fassent* ? Ensuite, combinez les méthodes existantes de manière novatrice afin que nous puissions nous rapprocher d'un monde juste et équitable, ludique et amusant, plus intelligent et plus compatissant.

Hay millones de formas de ganar una campaña. Los gráficos bien hechos pueden acelerar ese proceso, aunque es una estrategia creativa muy elemental. Muchos se centran en la táctica y la estética, pese a que sabemos por experiencia que los métodos tradicionales —una marcha, una ocupación, un boicot, una petición— se vuelven menos efectivos cada vez que se repiten. Por lo tanto, debemos plantearnos objetivos audaces y nuevas formas de alcanzarlos.

Una vez que tengas claro lo que esperas conseguir, deja que las inusuales combinaciones de imágenes que ves en estas páginas te sirvan de inspiración. Combina conceptos comunes y conocidos con ideas radicales e inusuales. Aglutina estos mensajes liberadores en conjuntos cómodos. Toma perspectivas complejas y transfórmalas en formas simples.

Este libro muestra algunas técnicas y ofrece muchos ejemplos. Puedes tomarlos prestados, recombinarlos con otros que ya conozcas, o desecharlos y desarrollar los tuyos propios. Recuerda, esos ejemplos no son el resultado. Este libro es sólo un punto de partida y, aunque puede resultarte gratificante tenerlo en tu colección, su papel no termina en el mero hecho de poseerlo. Puedes continuar lo que ha comenzado en estas páginas y activar las ideas combinándolas con las tuyas propias.

Considera ¿qué quieres que la gente piense? ¿Qué quieres que sientan? Y, lo más importante, ¿qué quieres *que hagan*? Luego, mezcla los métodos existentes de nuevas maneras que nos acerquen a un mundo justo y equitativo, lúdico y divertido, más inteligente y compasivo.

***

L'art est un pont qui relie des idées peu communes, idéalistes, voire radicales, à la vie quotidienne. Il est important de pouvoir rire tout en s'interrogeant activement sur les différentes structures de pouvoir à l'œuvre dans notre vie quotidienne.

***

***

El arte es un puente que conecta ideas inusuales, visionarias o incluso radicales con la vida cotidiana. Es importante ser capaz de reírte mientras cuestionas activamente las distintas estructuras de poder implicadas en nuestra vida cotidiana

***

PICTOSOPHY
LA PICTOSOPHIE
PICTOSOFIA

This book is a tribute to the graphic activist Gerd Arntz who, together with Otto and Marie Neurath, developed a non-verbal language with a strong conceptual and visual impact. It is also an homage to the artist and political activist Rini Templeton, who invited activists from all over the world to photocopy and use her 'Xerox Art' in their political struggles.

ARNTZ VARIATIONS XEROX ART & PICTOMONTAGE

VARIATIONS ARNTZ « ART XEROX » ET PICTOMONTAGE

VARIACIONES ARNTZ « XEROX ART » Y PICTOMONTAJES

SONIA & GABRIEL FREEMAN
—
2002 / 2020

Gerd Arntz's pictorial illustrations, applied through Isotype, are one of the most significant and influential examples of modern design.

'Variation' is a musical form of composition that allows different themes or musical ideas to be presented in an integrated way. To create a musical form, composers use two basic resources: repetition and contrast. The repetition of a musical idea can be literal or can present some alteration from the original idea. Variation is repetition of a theme, part, or motif with certain modifications (ornamentation of the melody, alteration of the harmony, rhythmic changes, etc.). In each variation, some essential aspects are always maintained, allowing it to be identified as a repetition of the original. The use of repetition as an activist tool, meanwhile, allows for the quick dissemination of images, as Rini Templeton showed us in the 1960s.

In graphic design, a visual variation is a composition characterized by one or more graphic themes, where each part is associated using conceptual patterns that give value to the visual whole. All variations you will find in this book have been developed using different themes by the *pictomontage* method.

Un Mundo Feliz
Spanish design project directed by Sonia Díaz and Gabriel Martínez. They aim to create and catalog reusable design elements in order to formulate common vocabulary for visual activism. —Josh MacPhee
—
projet de graphisme espagnol, dirigé par Sonia Díaz et Gabriel Martínez. Leur objectif est de créer et de répertorier des éléments graphiques réutilisables afin d'élaborer un vocabulaire commun pour l'activisme visuel. —Josh MacPhee
—
proyecto liderado por Sonia Díaz y Gabriel Martínez. Su objetivo es crear y catalogar elementos de diseño reutilizables con el fin de formular un vocabulario común para el activismo visual. —Josh MacPhee

>>> *gerdarntz.org*
>>> *riniart.com*
>>> *isotyperevisited.org*

ENG

Ce livre est un hommage au graphiste militant Gerd Arntz, qui, avec Otto et Marie Neurath, a inventé un langage non-verbal à fort impact conceptuel et visuel. C'est également un hommage à l'artiste et militante politique Rini Templeton, qui a invité des militants du monde entier à photocopier et à utiliser son « Xerox Art » dans leurs luttes politiques.

Les signes graphiques de Gerd Arntz, appelés Isotypes (International System of TYpographic Picture Education ou Système international d'éducation par les images typographiques), sont l'un des exemples les plus significatifs et influents du graphisme moderne.

La « variation » est une forme de composition musicale qui permet de présenter différents thèmes ou idées musicales de manière intégrée. Pour créer une forme musicale, les compositeurs utilisent deux ressources de base : la répétition et le contraste. La répétition d'une idée musicale peut être littérale ou peut présenter quelques altérations par rapport à l'idée originale. La variation est la répétition d'un thème, d'une partie ou d'un motif avec certaines modifications (ornement mélodique, altération harmonique, changements de rythme, etc.). Chaque variation conserve certains aspects essentiels, ainsi peut-on l'identifier comme une répétition de l'original. L'utilisation de la répétition comme outil militant permet de propager des images rapidement, comme nous l'a montré Rini Templeton dans les années 60.

En conception graphique, une variation visuelle est une composition caractérisée par un ou plusieurs thèmes graphiques, où chaque partie est associée par des motifs conceptuels qui mettent en valeur l'ensemble visuel. Toutes les variations que vous trouverez dans ce livre ont été développées à partir de différents thèmes, grâce à la méthode du *pictomontage*.

Este libro es un homenaje al activista gráfico Gerd Arntz que junto con Otto y Marie Neurath desarrollaron un lenguaje no verbal de fuerte impacto conceptual y visual. Y también a la artista y activista política Rini Templeton quien a través de su «Xerox Art» invitó a activistas de todo el mundo a fotocopiar y usar su trabajo para las luchas.

Las ilustraciones pictográficas de Gerd Arntz aplicadas a través de *Isotype* constituyen uno de los ejemplos más significativos e influyentes del diseño moderno.

La *variación* es una forma musical compositiva que permite presentar distintos temas o ideas musicales de manera integrada. Para crear una forma musical los compositores utilizan dos recursos básicos: la repetición y el contraste. La repetición de un concepto musical puede ser literal o presentar alguna alteración con respecto a la idea original. La variación es la repetición con ciertas modificaciones (ornamentación de la melodía, alteración de la armonía, cambios rítmicos, etc.) de un tema, parte o motivo. En cada variación siempre se mantienen algunos aspectos esenciales para poder identificarla como una repetición del original. Por otra parte, la utilización de la reiteración y la redundancia como herramientas activistas permite la diseminación rápida de las imágenes como bien nos enseñó Rini Templeton en los años 60.

En diseño gráfico una variación visual es una composición caracterizada por contener uno o varios temas gráficos donde cada parte se asocia utilizando patrones conceptuales que dan valor al conjunto visual. Las variaciones que encontrarás en este libro han sido construidas utilizando distintos temas mediante el *método de pictomontaje*.

FR

ES

PICTOSOPHY
LA PICTOSOPHIE
PICTOSOFIA

STEP
ÉTAPE
PASO

1

STEP
ÉTAPE
PASO

2

STEP
ÉTAPE
PASO

3

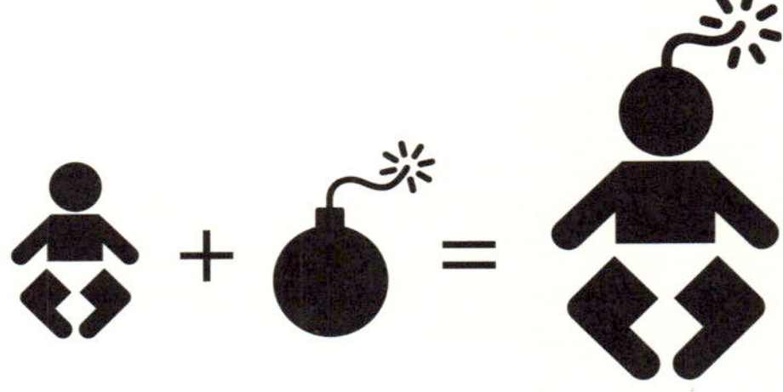

THE PICTOMONTAGE METHOD IN THREE STEPS

LA MÉTHODE DU PICTOMONTAGE EN TROIS ÉTAPES

EL MÉTODO DE PICTOMONTAJE EN TRES PASOS

The pictomontage method consists of juxtaposing binary pairs of visual code signs to 'cross over significant directions' (Buck-Morss). This operation has enormous semantic and critical force in questioning these signs. John Heartfield, through the technique of photomontage, developed this critical-dialectical idea using images and text. His principle of construction was the montage in which the elements that make up the image remain harmoniously unreconciled. Photomontages were not conceived as pure aesthetic objects, but as images to be read in a political sense. Pictosophy is an exercise in analysis and contextualization, in the search for meaning and the exchange of messages. The superficial appearance of the pictomontages is used as a gateway to a deeper reading of the image. For Un Mundo Feliz, design is a way of thinking that, to be visible, requires certain gestures. For that reason, we have always maintained that our images are acts of thought, with pictomontages their radical transmitters.

ENG

STEP
ÉTAPE
PASO

1

STEP
ÉTAPE
PASO

2

STEP
ÉTAPE
PASO

3

La méthode du pictomontage consiste à juxtaposer des signes binaires du code visuel pour que « des directions significatives se croisent » (Buck-Morss). Cette opération a une énorme force sémantique et critique dans la remise en question de ces signes. Grâce à la technique du photomontage, John Heartfield a développé cette idée critique-dialectique en utilisant des images et du texte. Son principe de construction était le montage, dans lequel les éléments qui composent l'image sont harmonieusement inconciliables. Les photomontages n'ont pas été conçus comme de simples objets esthétiques, mais comme des images ayant une interprétation politique. La *pictosophie* est un exercice d'analyse et de contextualisation, de recherche de sens et d'échange de messages. L'apparence superficielle des pictomontages sert de porte d'accès à une lecture plus profonde de l'image. Pour Un Mundo Feliz, prendre un crayon pour dessiner reflète une façon de penser qui, pour être visible, nécessite certains gestes. C'est pour cette raison que nous avons toujours soutenu que nos images sont des actes de pensée, les pictomontages étant leurs transmetteurs radicaux.

FR

El método de pictomontaje consiste en yuxtaponer pares binarios de signos del código visual para «cruzar direcciones significantes» (Buck-Morss). El poder crítico de esta maniobra posee una enorme fuerza semántica para poner en cuestión los signos. A través del fotomontaje John Heartfield desarrolló esta idea crítico-dialéctica utilizando imágenes y textos. Su principio de construcción es *el montaje,* donde los elementos que conforman la imagen permanecen armónicamente irreconciliados. Los fotomontajes no se idearon como meros objetos estéticos sino como imágenes para leer en un sentido político. *Pictosofía* es un ejercicio de análisis y contextualización, de busca de significados e intercambio de mensajes. La apariencia superficial de los *pictomontajes* se utiliza como puerta de acceso a una lectura más profunda de la imagen. Para Un Mundo Feliz diseñar es una manera de pensar que exige ciertos gestos que la evidencien, por esa razón, siempre hemos defendido que nuestras imágenes son actos de pensamiento y los *pictomontajes* su transmisor radical.

ES

PICTOSOPHY
LA PICTOSOPHIE
PICTOSOFÍA

AN ONGOING CONFLICT

UN CONFLIT PERMANENT

UN CONFLICTO PERMANENTE

S. & G. FREEMAN
(VS. SAUL ALINSKY)

The organizer's tactics
For Saul Alinsky, a tactic is to do what you can with what you have. It is the art of giving and taking. Every tactic is a determined and deliberate act that allows humankind to live together and in direct relation to the world around them. Tactics are specific applications of rules and principles; they are what the activist brings with him to the battlefield to put pressure on his enemies.

La tactique de l'organisateur
Pour Saul Alinsky, le mot « tactique » évoque l'idée de faire ce que l'on peut avec ce que l'on a. Les tactiques sont ces actes, choisis en connaissance de cause, qui permettent aux êtres humains de vivre ensemble et de traiter avec ce qui les entoure. C'est l'art de savoir comment prendre et comment donner. Les tactiques sont des applications spécifiques de règles et de principes ; c'est ce que l'activiste apporte avec lui sur le champ de bataille pour faire pression sur ses ennemis.

Las tácticas del organizador
Para Saul Alinsky una táctica es hacer lo que se puede con lo que se tiene. Es el arte de dar y tomar. Cada táctica es un acto decidido y deliberado que permite a los hombres vivir juntos y en relación directa con el mundo que les rodea. Las tácticas son aplicaciones específicas de las reglas y principios, y es lo que el activista lleva consigo al campo de batalla para presionar a sus enemigos.

Saul Alinsky
> *Rules for Radicals. A practical primer for realistic radicals*
> *Être radical : Manuel pragmatique pour radicaux réalistes*
> *Tratado para radicales. Manual para revolucionarios pragmáticos*

ENG / FR / ES

MANIPULATION (*rule 1*)
power is not only what
you have, but what the enemy
thinks you have

PROXIMITY (*rule 2*)
never go outside the expertise
of your people

FLEXIBILITY (*rule 3*)
whenever possible, go outside
the expertise of the enemy

FIDELITY [?] (*rule 4*)
make the enemy live up to
its own book of rules

IRREVERENCE (*rule 5*)
ridicule is man's most
potent weapon

FUN (*rule 6*)
a good tactic is one
your people enjoy

CHANGE (*rule 7*)
a tactic that drags on
too long becomes a drag

PRESSURE (*rule 8*)
keep the pressure on.
Never let up

THREAT (*rule 9*)
the threat is usually more
terrifying than the thing itself

CONSTANCY (*rule 10*)
the major premise for tactics
is the development of operations
that will maintain a constant
pressure upon the opposition

OPTIMISM (*rule 11*)
if you push a negative hard
enough, it will push through
and become a positive

CREATIVITY (*rule 12*)
the price of a successful attack
is a constructive alternative

APPROACH (*rule 13*)
pick the target, freeze it,
personalize it, and polarize it

LA MANIPULATION (*1ère règle*)
le pouvoir n'est pas seulement ce
que vous avez, mais également ce
que l'ennemi croit que vous avez

LA PROXIMITÉ (*2ème règle*)
ne sortez jamais du champ d'expérience
des gens de votre groupe

LA FLEXIBILITÉ (*3ème règle*)
sortez du champ d'expérience
de l'ennemi chaque fois que c'est
possible

LA FIDÉLITÉ [?] (*4ème règle*)
forcez l'ennemi à suivre à la lettre
son propre code de conduite

L'IRRÉVÉRENCE (*5ème règle*)
le ridicule est l'arme la plus
puissante dont l'homme dispose

LE PLAISIR (*6ème règle*)
une tactique n'est bonne que si vos
militants ont du plaisir à l'appliquer

LE CHANGEMENT (*7ème règle*)
une tactique qui traîne trop
en longueur devient pesante

LA PRESSION (*8ème règle*)
maintenez la pression, par
différentes tactiques ou opérations

LA MENACE (*9ème règle*)
la menace effraie généralement
davantage que l'action elle-même

LA CONSTANCE (*10ème règle*)
le principe fondamental d'une tactique,
c'est de faire en sorte que les événements
évoluent de façon à maintenir sur
l'opposition une pression permanente
qui provoquera des réactions

L'OPTIMISME (*11ème règle*)
en poussant suffisamment loin un
handicap, on en fait finalement un atout

LA CRÉATIVITÉ (*12ème règle*)
une attaque ne peut réussir que si
vous avez une solution de rechange
toute prête et constructive

L'APPROCHE (*13ème règle*)
il faut choisir sa cible, la figer,
la personnaliser, et polariser
l'attention sur elle au maximum

MANIPULACIÓN (*regla 1*)
el poder no es sólo lo que
tenéis, sino lo que el enemigo
cree que tenéis

CERCANÍA (*regla 2*)
no salgáis nunca del campo
de experiencias de vuestra gente

FLEXIBILIDAD (*regla 3*)
en cuanto podáis, salid del campo
de experiencia de vuestro enemigo

FIDELIDAD [?] (*regla 4*)
haced que el enemigo respete
su propio manual de reglas

IRREVERENCIA (*regla 5*)
el ridículo es el arma
más poderosa del hombre

DIVERSIÓN (*regla 6*)
una buena táctica es aquella
con la que tu gente disfruta

CAMBIO (*regla 7*)
una buena táctica que se alarga
demasiado en el tiempo
se convierte en aburrimiento

PRESIÓN (*regla 8*)
mantened la presión
(con acciones y tácticas diferentes)

AMENAZA (*regla 9*)
la amenaza es por lo general
mucho más terrorífica
que la propia acción

CONSTANCIA (*regla 10*)
la premisa mayor en el uso
de tácticas es que deben operar
manteniendo una presión
constante sobre la oposición

OPTIMISMO (*regla 11*)
si utilizas una desventaja
llevándola a su máxima expresión,
obtendrás una ventaja

CREATIVIDAD (*regla 12*)
el precio de un ataque con éxito
es una alternativa constructiva

ENFOQUE (*regla 13*)
elige el blanco, inmovilízalo,
personalízalo y polarízalo

PICTOSOPHY
LA PICTOSOPHIE
PICTOSOFIA

PROBLEMS IN ACTIVIST COMMUNICATION

LES PROBLÈMES DE COMMUNICATION DES MILITANTS

PROBLEMAS EN LA COMUNICACIÓN ACTIVISTA

S. & G. FREEMAN
(VS. ADRIANA AMADO)

Pop politics is the politics of serial communication.
—Adriana Amado

*La politique pop est la politique de communication
en série. . —Adriana Amado*

*La política pop es la política de la comunicación
en serie. —Adriana Amado*

This interaction is like a triangle whose vertices change according to the interests of the actors. The balance is broken when the relationships become closer or more distant, causing three vicious situations. ANESTHESIA: politicians and citizens do not receive critical messages, with the situation giving rise to conformism without commitment. SPECTACLE: designers lose their sense of confrontation and do commercial work; the result is aestheticisation and the loss of commitment. SECTARISM: when designers reproduce activist pseudo-messages, they are abducted by the system and put themselves at the service of power.

Cette interaction est représentée par un triangle dont les sommets changent selon les intérêts des acteurs. L'équilibre est rompu lorsque les relations deviennent plus étroites ou plus distantes, ce qui provoque trois situations en cercle vicieux. L'ANESTHÉSIE : les politiciens et les citoyens ne reçoivent pas de messages critiques, ce qui donne lieu à un conformisme sans engagement. Le SPECTACLE : les graphistes perdent l'esprit de confrontation et travaillent sur commandes ; le résultat est l'esthétisation et le désengagement. Le SECTARISME : lorsque les graphistes reproduisent des pseudo-messages militants, ils deviennent la proie du système et se mettent au service du pouvoir.

Esta interacción es como un triángulo cuyos vértices cambian según los intereses de los actores. El equilibrio se rompe cuando las relaciones se vuelven más cercanas o distantes provocando tres situaciones viciosas: ANESTESIA, políticos y ciudadanos no reciben mensajes críticos con las situaciones dando lugar a un conformismo sin compromiso. ESPECTÁCULO, los diseñadores pierden el sentido de confrontación y realizan trabajos comerciales; el resultado es una estetización y la pérdida del compromiso. SECTARISMO, cuando reproducen pseudomensajes activistas, son abducidos por el sistema y se ponen al servicio del poder.

ENG / FR / ES

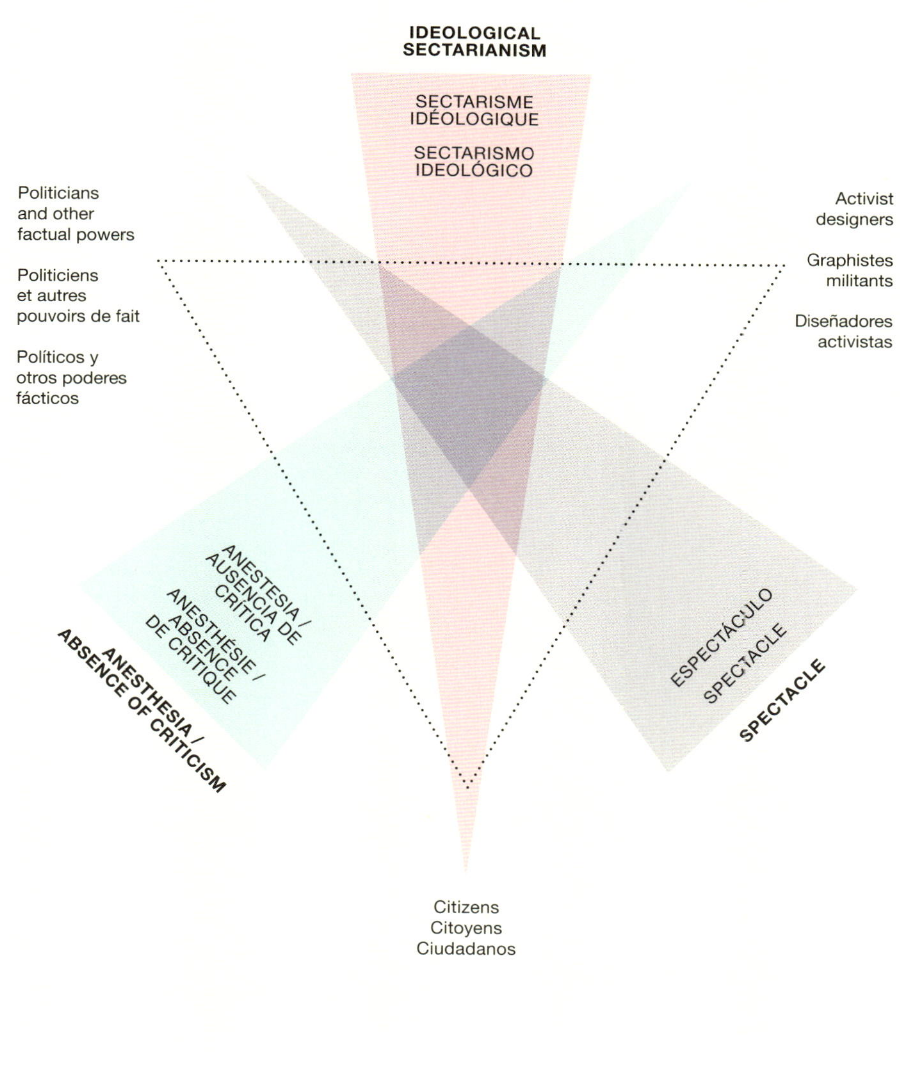

Political and activist actors in communication, and the imbalances in their ties

Les acteurs de la communication politique et militante et les déséquilibres existant dans leurs relations

Actores de la comunicación política y activista, y los desequilibrios en sus vínculos

PICTOSOPHY
LA PICTOSOPHIE
PICTOSOFÍA

ART, UTOPIA AND POLITICAL ACTION

ART, UTOPIE ET ACTION POLITIQUE

ARTE, UTOPIA Y ACCIÓN POLÍTICA

S. & G. FREEMAN
(VS. JULIA RAMÍREZ)

The problems of art in liberated space
Activist communication requires contextual
creativity. Julia Ramirez talks about an art of
the common that shares certain characteristics.
These images do not follow rules, but rather build
collectivity and are distinguished by immediacy
and appropriation. They like to provoke and are
open to the unexpected. Activist images are ways
of constructing the path, an essay of utopia,
and they therefore require continuous practice.

Les problèmes de l'art dans l'espace libéré
La communication militante exige une créativité
inséparable du contexte. Julia Ramirez parle
d'un art pour tous qui partage certaines
caractéristiques. Ces images ne suivent pas de
règles, mais renforcent plutôt la collectivité et se
distinguent par l'immédiateté et l'appropriation.
Elles aiment provoquer et sont ouvertes à
l'imprévu. Les images militantes servent à
tracer le chemin et font des exposés sur l'utopie ;
aussi requièrent-elles une pratique continue.

Los problemas del arte en el espacio liberado
La comunicación activista exige una creatividad
contextual. Según Julia Ramírez podríamos hablar
de un *arte del común* que comparte algunas
peculiaridades. Son imágenes que no siguen
normas, construyen colectividad y se caracterizan
por la inmediatez y la apropiación. Les gusta
la provocación y están abiertas a lo inesperado.
Las imágenes activistas son maneras de construir
el camino, un ensayo de la utopía y, por eso,
exigen una práctica continua.

>>> *juliaramirezblanco.com*

ENG / FR / ES

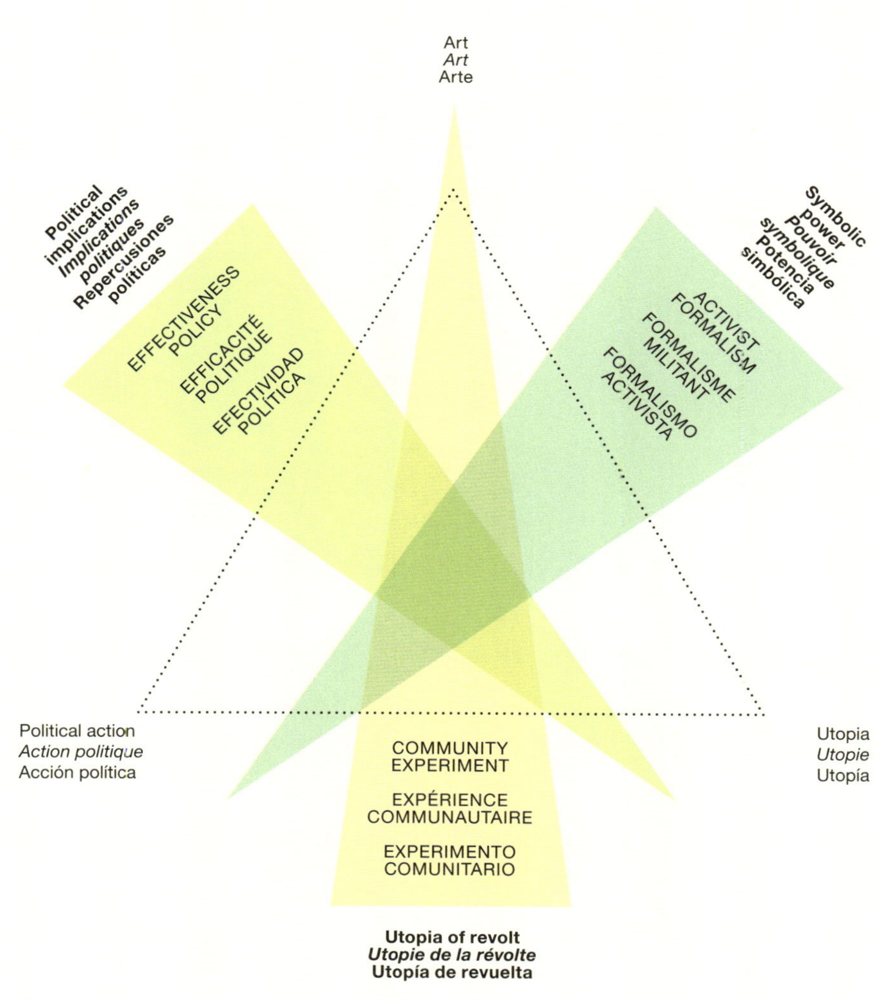

∧

∧

∧

Three forces in variable
equilibrium: symbolic power,
political effectiveness, and
the community experiment

Trois forces en équilibre
fluctuant : le pouvoir symbolique,
l'efficacité politique et
l'expérience communautaire

Tres fuerzas en equilibrio
variable: la potencia simbólica,
la efectividad política y
el experimento comunitario

PICTOSOPHY
LA PICTOSOPHIE
PICTOSOFIA

TACTICS AGAINST INJUSTICE

TACTIQUES CONTRE L'INJUSTICE

TÁCTICAS CONTRA LA INJUSTICIA

S. & G. FREEMAN
(VS. BRIAN MARTIN)

The backfire model is a framework for understanding tactics used by perpetrators of injustice and how to oppose them. When a powerful group does something unjust, it can take action to reduce popular outrage. But attacks sometimes backfire. They are counterproductive for the attackers. In fact, they are so disastrous for the attackers that they wish they had never done anything. Brian Martin offer five methods of reducing outrage and how they relate to an event, perceptions of it, and reactions to it.

Le *modèle de l'effet boomerang* offre un cadre permettant de comprendre les tactiques utilisées par les auteurs d'injustices et la manière de s'y opposer. Lorsqu'un groupe puissant commet une injustice, il utilise souvent certaines techniques pour réduire l'indignation populaire. Les attaques se retournent parfois contre leurs auteurs. Elles sont contreproductives pour les attaquants. Elles sont même tellement désastreuses pour les attaquants qu'ils souhaiteraient n'avoir rien fait. Brian Martin propose cinq techniques qui sont utilisées pour minimiser l'indignation et leur corrélation avec un événement, sa perception et les réactions provoquées.

El *modelo contraproducente* es un marco para comprender las tácticas utilizadas por los autores de la injusticia y cómo oponerse a ellas. Cuando un grupo poderoso hace algo injusto, puede tomar medidas para reducir la indignación popular. Pero los ataques a veces resultan contraproducentes. Son contraproducentes para los atacantes. De hecho, son tan desastrosos para los agresores que desearían no haber hecho nada. Brian Martin ofrece cinco métodos para reducir la indignación y analizar cómo se relacionan con un evento, las percepciones de éste y las reacciones ante él.

>>> bmartin.cc/pubs/backfire
>>> *nonviolent-conflict.org*

ENG / FR / ES

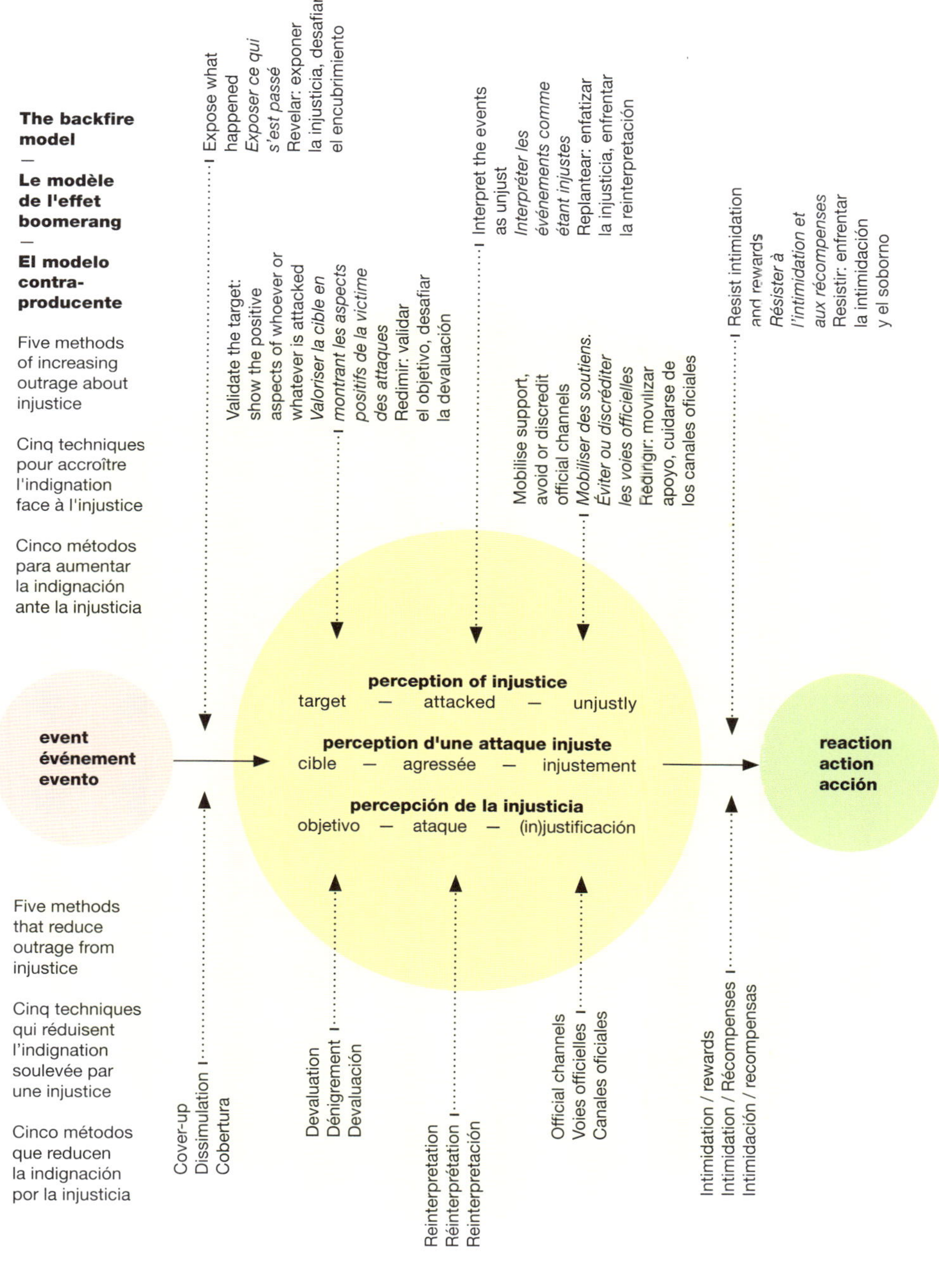

The backfire model
—
Le modèle de l'effet boomerang
—
El modelo contra-producente

Five methods of increasing outrage about injustice

Cinq techniques pour accroître l'indignation face à l'injustice

Cinco métodos para aumentar la indignación ante la injusticia

Five methods that reduce outrage from injustice

Cinq techniques qui réduisent l'indignation soulevée par une injustice

Cinco métodos que reducen la indignación por la injusticia

Expose what happened
Exposer ce qui s'est passé
Revelar: exponer la injusticia, desafiar el encubrimiento

Validate the target: show the positive aspects of whoever or whatever is attacked
Valoriser la cible en montrant les aspects positifs de la victime des attaques
Redimir: validar el objetivo, desafiar la devaluación

Interpret the events as unjust
Interpréter les événements comme étant injustes
Replantear: enfatizar la injusticia, enfrentar la reinterpretación

Mobilise support, avoid or discredit official channels
Mobiliser des soutiens. Éviter ou discréditer les voies officielles
Redirigir: movilizar apoyo, cuidarse de los canales oficiales

Resist intimidation and rewards
Résister à l'intimidation et aux récompenses
Resistir: enfrentar la intimidación y el soborno

Cover-up
Dissimulation
Cobertura

Devaluation
Dénigrement
Devaluación

Reinterpretation
Réinterprétation
Reinterpretación

Official channels
Voies officielles
Canales oficiales

Intimidation / rewards
Intimidation / Récompenses
Intimidación / recompensas

event
événement
evento

perception of injustice
target — attacked — unjustly

perception d'une attaque injuste
cible — agressée — injustement

percepción de la injusticia
objetivo — ataque — (in)justificación

reaction
action
acción

PICTOSOPHY
LA PICTOSOPHIE
PICTOSOFIA

SOCIALLY ENGAGED ART AND ETHICS

ART ENGAGÉ SOCIALEMENT ET ÉTHIQUE

ARTE SOCIALMENTE COMPROMETIDO Y ÉTICA

S. & G. FREEMAN
(VS. PABLO HELGUERA
BRIAN HOLMES &
GEORGE KATSIAFICAS)

Honesty and openness are important in establishing relationships of trust, and trust is key when engaging in productive activities with others. Artistic activism is an affectivism that opens and expands territories, from the intimate relationship to the wild embrace of the crowd. The Eros Effect is the sudden awakening of solidarity and mass opposition to the established system.

L'honnêteté et l'ouverture d'esprit sont importantes pour établir des relations de confiance et la confiance est essentielle lorsque l'on s'engage dans des activités productives avec d'autres. L'activisme artistique est un affectivisme qui ouvre et élargit les horizons, de la relation intime à l'étreinte passionnée de la foule. L'effet Eros est le réveil soudain de la solidarité et de l'opposition de masse au système établi.

La honestidad y la franqueza son importantes en el establecimiento de relaciones de confianza; y la confianza es la clave cuando se participa en actividades productivas con otros. El activismo artístico es un *afectivismo* que abre y expande territorios que van de la relación íntima al abrazo salvaje de la muchedumbre. El *Efecto Eros* es el despertar repentino de la solidaridad y de la oposición masiva al sistema establecido.

>>> *pablohelguera.net*
>>> *brianholmes.wordpress.com*
>>> *eroseffect.com*

ENG / FR / ES

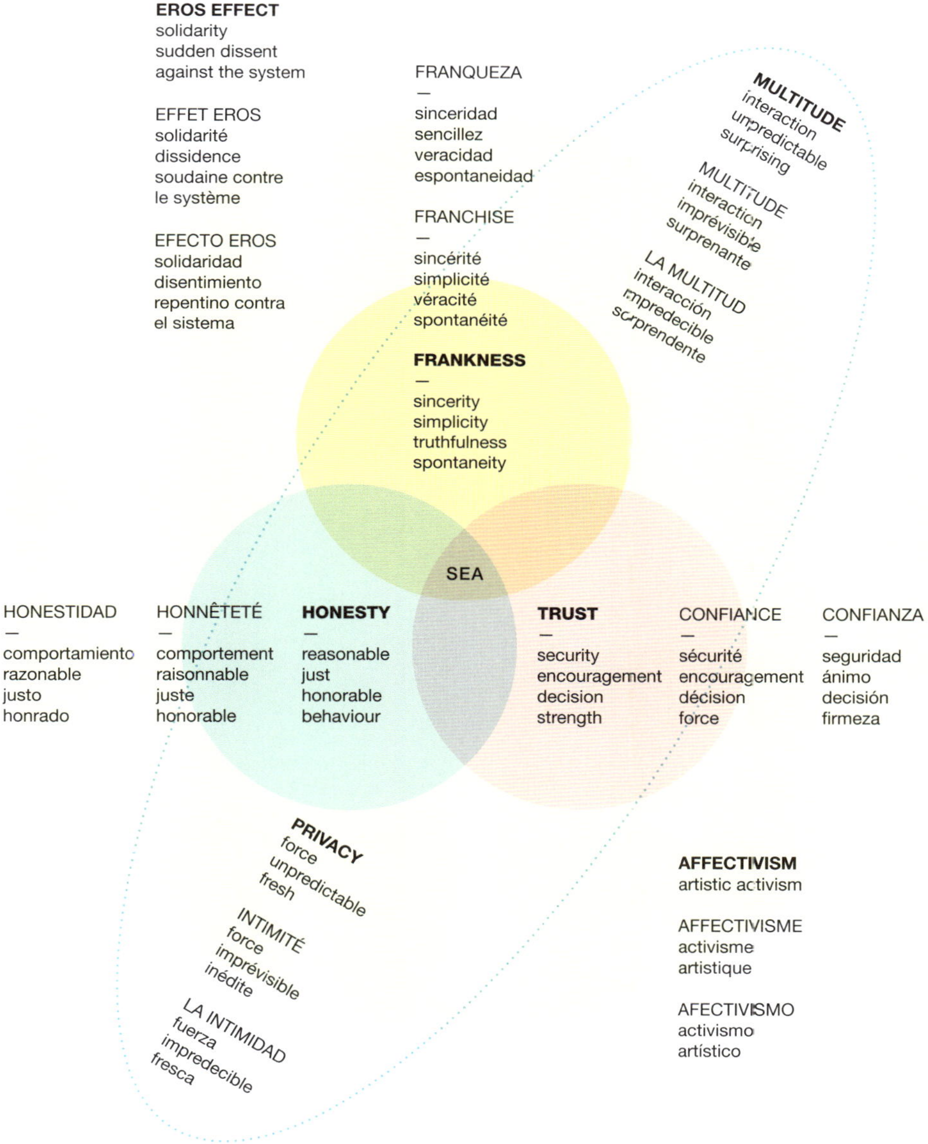

∧
SEA /
Social Engaged Art

∧
SEA / Social Engaged Art =
Art engagé socialement

∧
SEA / Social Engaged Art =
Arte socialmente comprometido

PICTOSOPHY
LA PICTOSOPHIE
PICTOSOFIA

I thought graphic design was worth doing partly because I saw it as a political activity. I came to this conclusion as a student. —Lucienne Roberts

Selon moi, être graphiste en valait la peine, en partie parce que je considérais le graphisme comme une activité politique. Je suis arrivée à cette conclusion pendant mes études. —Lucienne Roberts

Pensé que valía la pena dedicarme al diseño gráfico en parte porque lo veía como una actividad política. Llegué a esta conclusión cuando estudiaba. —Lucienne Roberts

OUTLINES OF AN ACTIVIST PRACTICE

LES GRANDES LIGNES D'UNE PRATIQUE MILITANTE

ESQUEMAS DE UNA PRÁCTICA ACTIVISTA

Graphic activism is an aesthetic tool for action, causing a short circuit that suddenly increases the intensity of autonomous, social, and cultural communication through creative strategies.

L'activisme graphique est un outil d'action esthétique qui, par le biais de stratégies créatives, produit un court-circuit, qui augmente soudainement l'intensité de la communication autonome, sociale et culturelle.

El activismo gráfico es una herramienta estética de acción que, a través de estrategias creativas, produce un cortocircuito que aumenta de manera repentina la intensidad de la comunicación autónoma, social y cultural.

ENG / FR / ES

Affectivism (Brian Holmes) + Pleasure-Politics (Tim Jordan) + Depropiation (Marcus Boon) + Eros Effect (George Katsiaficas) + TAZ / Temporary Autonomous Zone (Hakim Bey) + Active Time (Stine Krøijer) + Activist Constructivism (Alberto Melucci)

A creative statement / It is *affectivist*, an artistic activism that fights to defend the hearts and minds of people. It is a useful art, one that plays a role in the political process by providing society with an alternative cultural model, where freedom and justice override the capitalist consumer aesthetic. Its aesthetics are appropriated, lawless, and often produced in a communitarian and anonymous way. Over time, its iconography has served to build a value system based on a political, social, and cultural awareness of conflict. **[Which builds] a provisional network** / It is activist *constructivism*. It creates a social, emotional, and supportive identity. Activist images that occupy public space are pictures that feed and build that space. Thanks to ICTs, paths of creation and collective action are even more visible and accessible, creating a multiple, elastic, and provisional pseudo-system.

Collective-participatory / It causes a temporary autonomous zone (TAZ), which activates the time of participation. It can be the responsibility of a single designer or artist, but its purpose is to provide value to the group. It is an individual expression but is felt as belonging to a larger autonomous community or unit. **Politics** / It is pleasure-politics, a social practice that takes place in the context of everyday life and deals with burning issues in society – identity, rights, values, representation – using messages that the average citizen easily grasps and acting as an agent of social change by sensitizing individuals and institutions. **Multiple** / It is depropriation, a design of designs with multiple and heterogeneous messages in its form and subject matter. It is process-oriented, its repertoire making litigious collective action issues visible through ephemeral works. Beyond having an aesthetic concern, it seeks freedom of collective expression and builds new revolutionary aesthetic sensibilities. **Persuasive** / It is moved by the *Eros Effect*, an intuitive force of solidarity and dissidence. Every self-respecting visual activism project tries to influence others by using the power of image and word. It is a strategic and tactical counter-manipulation that works as a response to a previous manipulation, trying to change a message by providing new readings Visual activism rebels against strong strategies by promoting weak but extended strategies that allow fluid responses to everyday needs. Its objectives are social, not aesthetic. It seeks to provoke courageous cultural and political agitation.

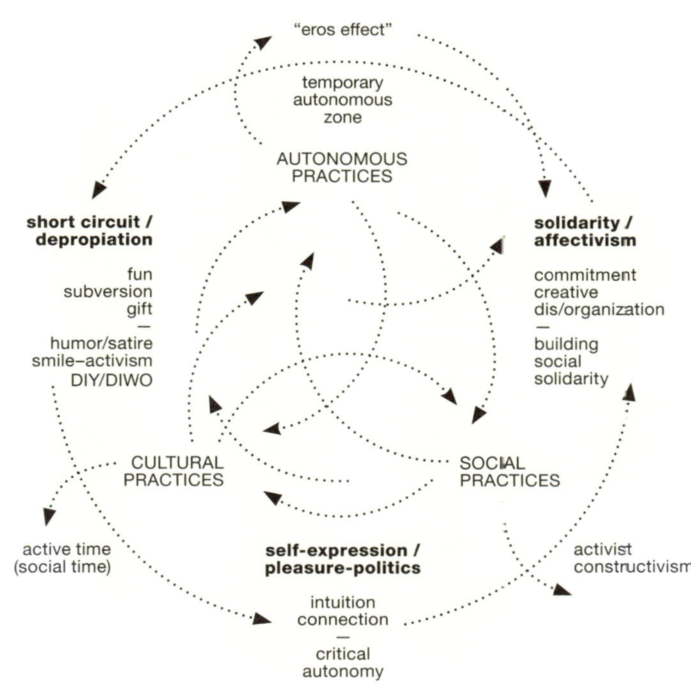

ENG

Une déclaration créative / C'est de *l'affectivisme*, un activisme artistique qui se bat pour défendre le cœur et l'esprit des gens. C'est un art utile, qui joue un rôle dans le processus politique en proposant à la société un modèle culturel alternatif, où la liberté et la justice prévalent sur l'esthétique de la consommation capitaliste. Son esthétique est appropriée, anarchique et souvent créée de manière collective et anonyme. Au fil du temps, son iconographie a servi à construire un système de valeurs basé sur une conscience politique, sociale et culturelle du conflit. **[Qui construit] un réseau provisoire** / C'est du *constructivisme* militant. Il crée une identité sociale, émotionnelle et solidaire. Les images militantes occupant l'espace public sont des images qui nourrissent et construisent cet espace. Grâce aux technologies de l'information et de la communication (TIC), les voies de la création et de l'action collective sont encore plus visibles et accessibles et créent un pseudo-système multiple, souple et provisoire. **Collective-participative** / elle génère une zone autonome temporaire (Temporary Autonomous Zone ou TAZ), qui déclenche le temps de participation. Elle peut relever d'un seul concepteur ou d'un seul artiste, mais son objectif est de valoriser le groupe. Il s'agit d'une expression individuelle qui, toutefois, est ressentie comme appartenant à une communauté ou à une unité autonome plus large. **Politique** / C'est le plaisir-politique, une pratique sociale qui s'inscrit dans le contexte de la vie quotidienne et qui se penche sur les questions brûlantes de la société - identité, droits, valeurs, représentation -, en utilisant des messages que le citoyen moyen peut facilement comprendre et en intervenant en tant qu'agent de changement social par la sensibilisation des individus et des institutions. **Multiple** / C'est de la « dépropriation », une conception graphique contenant des messages multiples et hétérogènes quant à leur forme et à leur objet. Elle est axée sur le processus, son répertoire rend visibles les enjeux controversés de l'action collective à travers des œuvres éphémères. Au-delà d'un souci esthétique, elle recherche la liberté d'expression collective et construit de nouvelles sensibilités esthétiques révolutionnaires. **Persuasive** / Elle est animée par *l'Effet Eros*, une force intuitive de solidarité et de dissidence. Tout projet d'activisme visuel qui se respecte tente d'influencer les autres en utilisant le pouvoir de l'image et de la parole. Il s'agit d'une contre-manipulation stratégique et tactique qui fait office de réaction à une manipulation précédente, en essayant de changer un message par la proposition de nouvelles lectures. L'activisme visuel se rebelle contre les stratégies fortes en promouvant des stratégies faibles, mais élargies, qui permettent de donner une réponse fluide aux besoins quotidiens. Ses objectifs sont sociaux et pas esthétiques. Il vise à provoquer une agitation culturelle et politique courageuse.

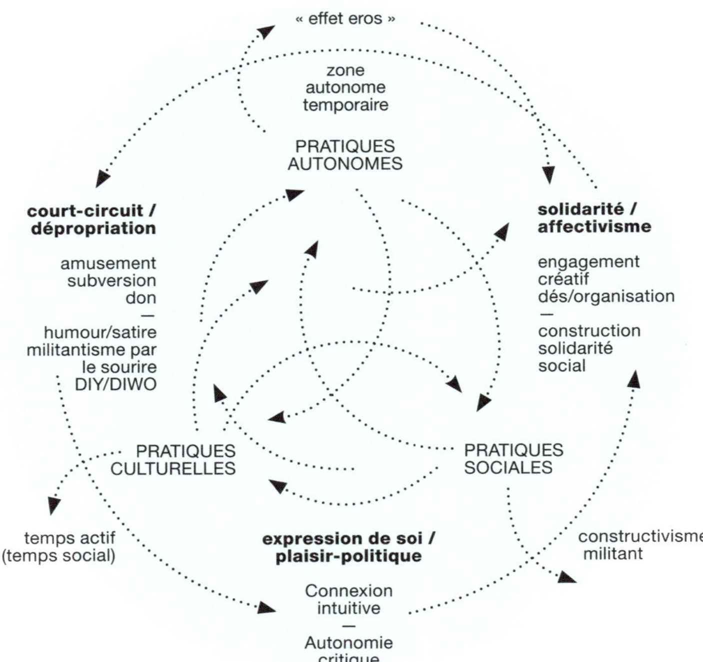

Affectivisme (Brian Holmes) + Plaisir-Politique (Tim Jordan) + Dépropriation (Marcus Boon) + Effet Eros (George Katsiaficas) + TAZ / Zone Autonome Temporaire (Hakim Bey) + Temps actif (Stine Krøjer) + Constructivisme activiste (Alberto Melucci)

FR

Una manifestación creativa / Es afectivista, un activismo artístico que lucha por defender los corazones y las mentes de las personas. Es un arte útil porque ejerce un papel en el proceso político aportando a la sociedad un modelo cultural alternativo donde libertad y justicia prevalecen sobre la estética de consumo capitalista. Su estética es apropiacionista, anárquica y, muchas veces, producida de forma comunitaria y anónima. A lo largo del tiempo, su iconografía ha servido para construir un sistema de valores basado en una consciencia política, social y cultural de los conflictos.

[Que construye] una red provisional / Es constructivismo activista. Crea una identidad social, emocional y solidaria. Las imágenes activistas que ocupan el espacio público son imágenes que alimentan y construyen ese espacio. Gracias a las TIC, las formas de creación y acción colectiva son aún más visibles y accesibles, y crean un pseudosistema múltiple, elástico y provisional. **Colectiva-participativa** / Provoca una zona autónoma temporal (TAZ) que activa el tiempo de participación. Puede ser responsabilidad de un solo diseñador o artista pero su sentido es aportar valor al grupo. Es una expresión individual pero sentida como perteneciente a una comunidad o unidad mayor autónoma. **Política** / Es placer-política, una práctica social que tiene lugar en el contexto de la vida cotidiana y trata sobre temas candentes en la sociedad —identidad, derechos, valores, representación—, utiliza mensajes que el ciudadano medio capta fácilmente y actúa como un agente de cambio social sensibilizando a individuos e instituciones.

Múltiple / Es depropiación, un diseño-de-diseños con mensajes múltiples y heterogéneos en su forma y temática. Está orientado al proceso y su repertorio visibiliza problemáticas de acción colectiva contenciosas a través de obras efímeras. Más allá de tener una preocupación estética busca la libertad de expresión colectiva y construye nuevas sensibilidades estéticas revolucionarias.

Persuasiva / Se mueve por el «efecto eros», una fuerza intuitiva solidaria y disidente. Todo proyecto de activismo visual que se precie intenta influir en los demás utilizando la fuerza de la imagen y de la palabra. Es una contra-manipulación estratégica y táctica que funciona como respuesta a una manipulación anterior e intenta cambiar un mensaje proporcionando nuevas lecturas. El activismo visual se rebela contra las «estrategias fuertes» promoviendo estrategias «débiles pero extendidas» que permiten respuestas fluidas a necesidades cotidianas. Sus objetivos son sociales, no estéticos. Busca provocar una agitación cultural y política valiente.

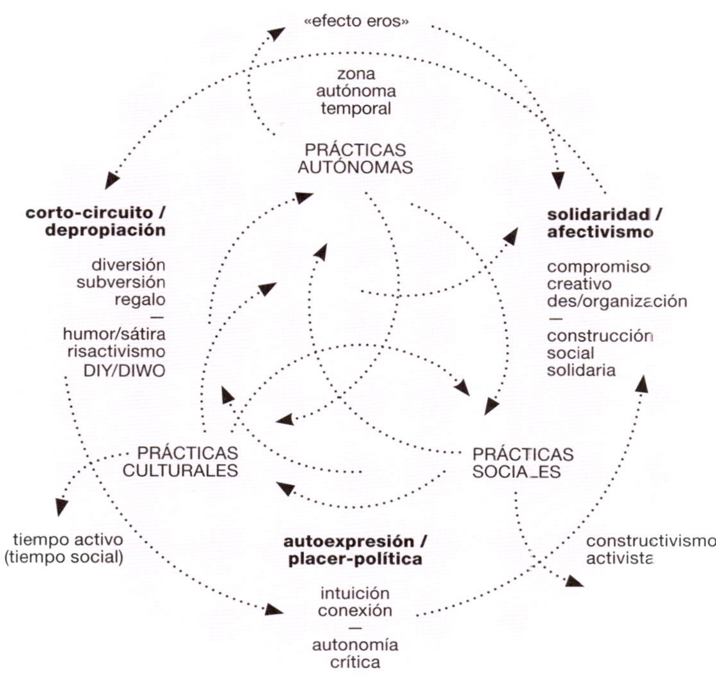

+ Efecto Eros (George Katsiaficas) + TAZ / Zona Autónoma Temporal (Hakim Bey)
+ Tiempo Activo (Stine Krøijer) + Activismo Constructivista (Alberto Melucci)

ES

1

Write a manifesto. Draw up a public statement of purpose
To build interest and spread our ideas, we produce a cheap and simple product: a fanzine.

—

Rédiger un manifeste. Faire une déclaration publique d'intention
Pour susciter l'intérêt et diffuser nos idées, nous utilisons un média simple et bon marché : le fanzine.

—

Redactar un manifiesto. Hacer una declaración pública de intenciones
Para crear interés y divulgar nuestras ideas utilizamos un medio barato y sencillo de producir: un fanzine.

2

Publish a message: design as a communication exercise in the name of nonviolence
Gene Sharp, *The Politics of Nonviolent Action,* and part two, *The Methods of Nonviolent Action.*

—

Publier un message : le graphisme comme exercice de communication au service de la non-violence
Gene Sharp. *198 Méthodes d'Action non violentes. Méthodes de protestation et de persuasion non-violentes.*

—

Editar/publicar un mensaje: el diseño como un ejercicio de comunicación al servicio de la *noviolencia*
Gene Sharp. *198 Maneras de actuar. Métodos de protesta y persuasión noviolentos.*

3

Disseminate/construct 'an alternative story'
Designed posters on Matilde Landa and the Maquis, to promote and consolidate international activist culture.

—

Diffuser/construire « une histoire alternative »
Réalisation d'affiches sur Matilde Landa et le Maquis, afin de promouvoir et de consolider la culture militante internationale.

—

Difundir/construir «otra historia»
Carteles sobre Matilde Landa y el Maquis diseñados para promocionar y consolidar la cultura activista internacional.

4

Dress to speak out
T-shirt design is an everyday practice that can make a difference.

—

S'habiller pour se faire entendre
La conception de t-shirts est une pratique quotidienne qui peut changer les choses.

—

Vestirse para opinar
El diseño de camisetas es un ejercicio cotidiano que puede marcar la diferencia.

5

Create a slogan, design a fake
Fakes are subvertising exercises. Their power lies in recognition of the motif and the play that occurs when the meaning is modified. A fake is a visual joke.

—

Créer un slogan, réaliser un faux
Les imitations sont des exercices subversifs. Leur pouvoir réside dans la reconnaissance du motif et du jeu créé lorsque le sens est modifié. Un faux est un canular visuel.

—

Acuñar un eslogan, diseñar un *fake*
Los *fakes* son ejercicios de *subvertising.* Su potencia radica en poder reconocer el motivo y el juego que se produce al cambiar el significado. Un *fake* es un chiste visual.

Bold n.1
Pictopia Stencil
Fanzine
2008

Sazmindat /
Boldbooks
A6 Fanzine
2012

Two posters for
Celebrate People's
History / Deux
affiches pour
célébrer l'histoire
du peuple /
Interference
Archive

Jour de la Terre
Canadian NGO
+
Occupy /
Occuprint

Ray-Ban Fake
In Spanish *Roban*
means *They steal* /
En espagnol, *Roban*
signifie *Ils volent* /
En espagnol, Roban
signifie Ils volent

**PICTOSOPHY
LA PICTOSOPHIE
PICTOSOFIA**

6

Use the power of speech

The designed word has two times the power of the spoken word. Political Types is about establishing an engagement with the message.

—

Utiliser le pouvoir de la parole

Le mot dessiné est doublement plus puissant que celui prononcé. Il s'agit d'un engagement politique par le biais du message.

—

Utilizar la fuerza de palabra

La palabra diseñada tiene el doble de potencia que la palabra pronunciada. Political Types consiste en establecer un compromiso con el mensaje.

7

Stage a party: celebrate the protest

Party demonstrations are a time of celebration, a way of building community and sharing a common passion in public space.

—

Organiser une fête : célébrer la protestation

Les manifestations festives sont des moments de célébration, une manière de construire une communauté et de partager une passion commune dans l'espace public.

—

Montar una fiesta: celebrar la protesta

Las manifestaciones festivas son una celebración, una forma de hacer comunidad y de compartir intereses en el espacio público.

8

Disguise yourself symbolically

The festive strategy seeks to create a sense of interest, establish commitments, and consolidate emotional relationships among all participants.

—

Se déguiser symboliquement

L'esprit festif d'un événement fait partie d'une stratégie qui vise à susciter l'intérêt, à prendre des engagements et à consolider les relations émotionnelles entre tous les participants.

—

Disfrazarse simbólicamente

La estrategia festiva busca crear interés, establecer compromisos y consolidar relaciones emocionales entre los participantes.

9

Write a book, publish a newspaper

When you write, design, or print a book, you can reach many more people. A book is a good tool because it never goes out of date.

—

Écrire un livre, publier un journal

Lorsque vous concevez, vous rédigez et vous publiez un livre, vous pouvez toucher un plus grand nombre de personnes. Un livre est un bon outil, car il ne passe jamais de mode.

—

Escribir un libro, publicar un periódico

Cuando escribes, diseñas o editas un libro tienes la oportunidad de llegar a mucha más gente. Un libro es una buena herramienta porque nunca pasa de moda.

10

Repeat, repeat, repeat

Don't get tired of repetition. Something new and exciting always happens when you repeat an action or a design.

—

Répéter, répéter, répéter

Ne vous lassez pas des répétitions. Il se passe toujours quelque chose de nouveau et d'excitant en répétant une action ou en reproduisant un dessin.

—

Repetir, repetir, repetir

No te canses de repetir. Cuando repites una acción o un diseño siempre se produce algo nuevo y excitante.

Political Types Postcards & posters / Caractères politiques Cartes postales et affiches / Carteles y postales 2005—2020

Public education protests / Protestations de l'enseignement public / Protestas por la educación pública

Protests against public cutbacks / Protestations contre les coupes budgétaires / Protestas contra los recortes públicos

Pictopia Promopress 2008

Woman Sans Minchó Press 2020

10 STRATEGIES AND TACTICS

10 STRATÉGIES ET TACTIQUES

10 ESTRATEGIAS Y TÁCTICAS

Anti
LIFE

Design is inevitably political, in that it includes an element of hope — a dream, however vague, containing the outlines of the society we want to live in.
—Gui Bonsiepe

Le dessin est inévitablement politique, en ce sens qu'il comporte un élément d'espoir - un rêve, aussi vague soit-il, définissant les contours de la société dans laquelle nous voulons vivre.
—Gui Bonsiepe

El diseño es inevitablemente político, porque comprende un componente de esperanza: el sueño aunque vago de una sociedad más digna de vivirse.
—Gui Bonsiepe

1

2

3

4

5 *

6

7

8

9

***Tea Party** / is a right-wing American political movement focused on fiscally conservative politics and defined by originalism – that is, by a return to the philosophical-constitutional origins of the United States.

***Tea Party** / un mouvement politique américain de droite axé sur une politique financièrement conservatrice et préconisant l'originalisme - c'est-à-dire un retour aux origines philosophiques et constitutionnelles des États-Unis.

***Tea Party** / es un movimiento político estadounidense de derecha centrado en una política fiscalmente conservadora, y definido por el originalismo, es decir, la vuelta a los orígenes filosófico-constitucionales de los Estados Unidos.

UN MUNDO FELIZ

THE MIGRATION ISSUE
LA QUESTION MIGRATOIRE

11

12

13

14

15

16 *

17

18

19

***Mexico '68** / during 'The Games of Peace', a student confrontation began that led to the October 2 massacre in Tlatelolco. The present protest graphic has its origins in the work of *Taller de Gráfica Popular.*

***Mexique 68** / pendant les « Jeux de la Paix », des manifestations d'étudiants et des affrontements ont débouché sur le massacre du 2 octobre à Tlatelolco. Ce graphisme de protestation trouve son origine dans l'œuvre de l'atelier *Taller de Gráfica Popular.*

***México '68** / durante «Los Juegos de la Paz» se inició una confrontación estudiantil que desembocó en la matanza del 2 de octubre en Tlatelolco. La gráfica de protesta del momento tiene sus antecedentes en el trabajo del Taller de Gráfica Popular.

20

21

22

23

24

25

26

27 *

28

***Otpor!** / (Resistance!) was a pro-
democratic youth movement in Serbia
that developed an intense campaign
to oust Slobodan Milosevic from
power. It has promoted other youth
movements and is now considered
an 'exporter of revolutions'.

***Otpor !** / (Résistance !) était
un mouvement de jeunesse serbe
pro-démocratique qui a mené une
campagne véhémente contre le régime
de Slobodan Milosevic. Il a encouragé
d'autres mouvements de jeunesse
et est aujourd'hui considéré comme
un « exportateur de révolutions ».

***Otpor!** / (¡Resistancia!) fue un
movimiento juvenil prodemocrático
en Serbia que desarrolló una intensa
campaña para expulsar del poder a
Slobodan Milósevic. Han impulsado
otros movimientos juveniles y se
les considera «exportadores de
revoluciones».

29

30

31

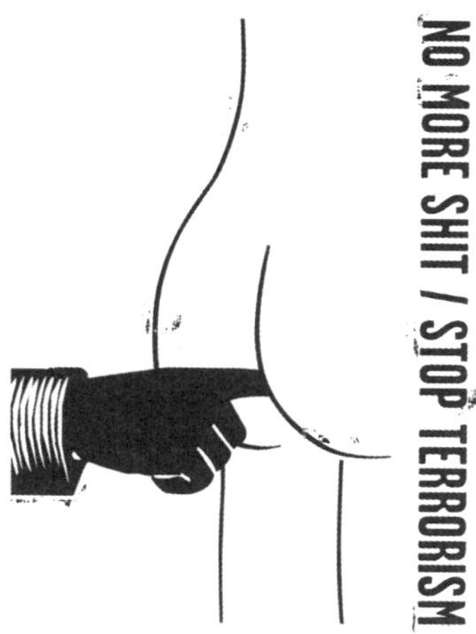

32

Unicode reserves character U+1F480 for a human skull pictogram.

Le code **Unicode** U+1F480 correspond au pictogramme du crâne humain.

Unicode reserva el carácter U+1F480 para un picto del cráneo humano.

***La Catrina** / was a character
created by José Guadalupe Posada.
These drawings of skulls and skeletons
portrayed the misery, political errors,
and hypocrisy of society. They
accompanied satirical writings in
newspapers, entitled 'Combat'.

***La Catrina** / est un personnage
créé par José Guadalupe Posada.
Il s'agissait de dessins de crânes et de
squelettes qui dépeignaient la misère,
les erreurs politiques et l'hypocrisie
de la société. Ils accompagnaient des
textes satiriques dans les journaux,
intitulés « de combat ».

***La Catrina** / es una figura creada
por José Guadalupe Posada. Eran
dibujos de cráneos y esqueletos
que retrataban la miseria, los errores
políticos y la hipocresía de la sociedad
y acompañaban escritos satíricos en
periódicos llamados «de combate».

35

36

37

38

39 *

40

41

42

43

***The Animal Rights Movement** /
also known as the animal liberation
movement. It seeks an end to the moral
and legal distinction drawn between
human and non-human animals, an end
to the status of animals as property,
and an end to their use in industry.

***Le Mouvement de défense des
droits des animaux** / également connu
sous le nom de Mouvement de libération
des animaux tente d'abolir la distinction
morale et juridique établie entre les espèces
animales humaines et non humaines et
de mettre fin au statut de propriété des
animaux et à leur utilisation dans l'industrie.

***El Movimiento por los Derechos
de los Animales** / o movimiento
de liberación de los animales busca
el fin de la distinción moral y legal que
se hace entre los animales humanos
y no humanos, el fin del estatus
de los animales como propiedad
y el fin de su uso en las industrias.

44

45

46

47

48

49

50

51

52

53

54

55

56

57
....

58
....

59
....

60
....

61 *
....

62
....

63
....

*Occupy / was a socio-political movement that expressed opposition to social and economic inequality and to the lack of 'real democracy' around the world. / **Occuprint** collects, prints, and distributes posters from the movement.

64
....

*Occupy / un mouvement socio-politique exprimant son opposition aux inégalités sociales et économiques et à l'absence de « démocratie réelle » dans le monde. / **Occuprint** collecte, imprime et distribue des affiches du mouvement.

65
....

*Occupy / fue un movimiento sociopolítico que expresó su oposición a la desigualdad social y económica y a la falta de «democracia real» en todo el mundo. / **Occuprint** colecciona, imprime y distribuye carteles del movimiento.

66

67

68 *

69

Butterflies / the Mirabal Sisters, also known as Las Mirabal or Mariposas (Patria, Minerva, María Teresa, and Dedé Mirabal), were four Dominican women who opposed the dictatorship of Rafael Leónidas Trujillo. Three of them were murdered on November 25, 1960.

Les Papillons / les Sœurs Mirabal, aussi connues sous le nom de Las Mirabal ou Mariposas (Patria, Minerva, María Teresa et Dedé Mirabal), étaient quatre Dominicaines qui s'opposèrent au régime dictatorial de Rafael Leónidas Trujillo. Trois d'entre elles furent assassinées le 25 novembre 1960.

Mariposas / las Hermanas Mirabal, también conocidas como Las Mirabal o Mariposas (Patria, Minerva, María Teresa y Dedé Mirabal), fueron cuatro mujeres dominicanas que se opusieron a la dictadura de Rafael Leónidas Trujillo. Tres de ellas fueron asesinadas el 25 de noviembre de 1960.

PEOPLE

BANKS

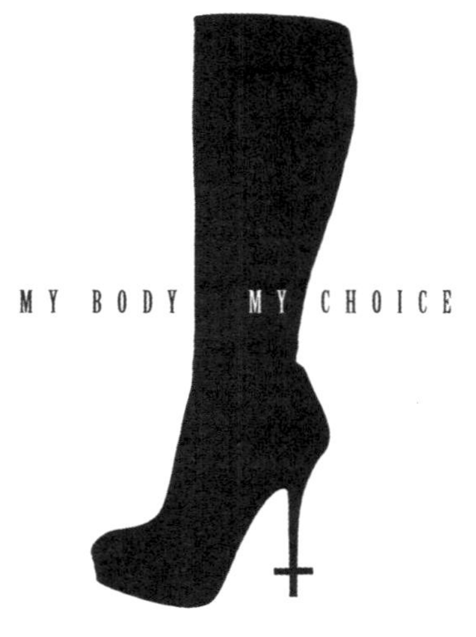

70

71

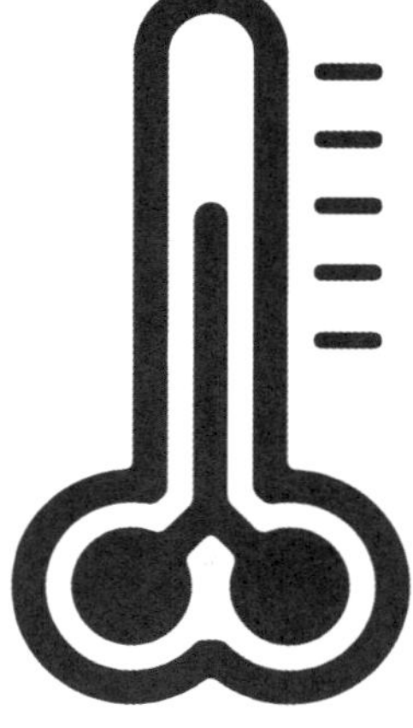

72

73

***Make Love Not War** / Diane Newell
Meyer, a student at the University of
Oregon in 1965, says she wrote 'Let's
make love not war' on an envelope
and pinned it to her sweater before
attending a rally in April 1965.

***Faites l'amour, pas la guerre** /
Diane Newell Meyer, étudiante à
l'université de l'Oregon en 1965,
raconte qu'elle a épinglé le slogan
« Let's make love not war » sur
son pull avant d'assister à une
manifestation en avril 1965.

***Haz el amor, no la guerra** /
Diane Newell Meyer, estudiante de
la Universidad de Oregón en 1965,
cuenta que escribió «Let's make love
not war» en un sobre y lo pegó a su
suéter antes de asistir a un mitin
en abril de 1965.

October 25, 2005
Rosa Parks, the woman known as the "mother of the civil rights movement," has died. Parks turned the course of American history by refusing in 1955 to give up her seat on a bus for a white man.

CIVIL RIGHTS HUMAN RIGHTS

MY CHOICE

PROTEST PICTOGRAM ACTIVISM

76 *

***PAH** / (Platform of People Affected by Mortgages) is a citizens' movement that was born in Barcelona. It brings together activists who want to make the right to housing effective for all citizens.

***PAH** / *Plataforma de Afectados por la Hipoteca* / (La Plate-forme des victimes du crédit hypothécaire) est un mouvement citoyen né à Barcelone, rassemblant des militants qui luttent pour rendre effectif le droit au logement pour tous.

***PAH** / (Plataforma de Afectados por la Hipoteca) es un movimiento ciudadano que nació en Barcelona y agrupa a activistas solidarios que quieren hacer efectivo el derecho a la vivienda para toda la ciudadanía.

77

78

79

80

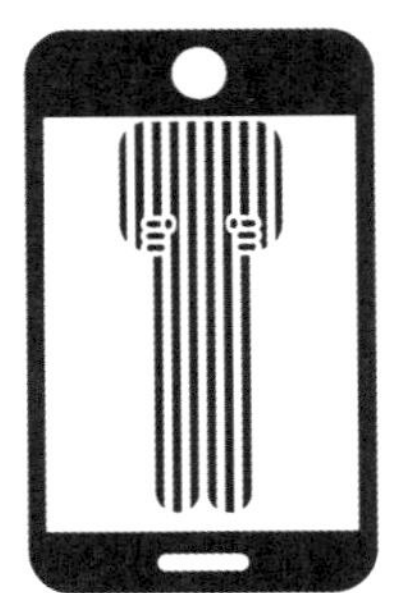

81

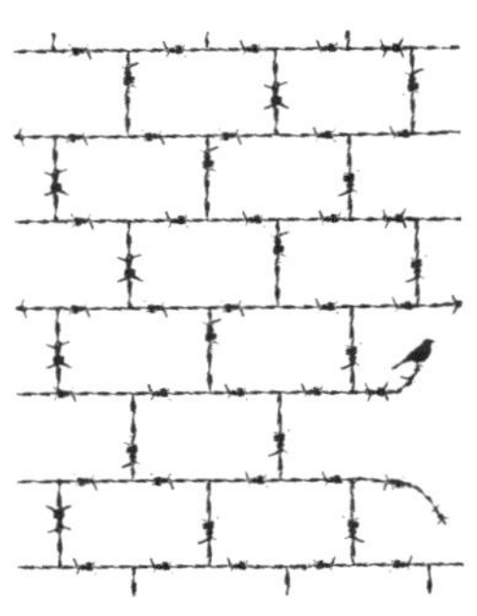

82

83

84

85 *

***Arab Spring** / was a series of anti-government protests, uprisings, and rebellions that spread across much of the Arab world in the early 2010s in response to oppressive regimes and a low standard of living.

***Le Printemps Arabe** / était un ensemble de protestations populaires, de rébellions et de soulèvements anti-gouvernementaux, qui se sont répandus dans une grande partie du monde arabe au début des années 2010, en réaction aux régimes oppressifs et à un faible niveau de vie.

***Primavera Árabe** / fue una serie de protestas, levantamientos y rebeliones antigubernamentales que se extendieron por gran parte del mundo árabe a principios de la década de 2010 en respuesta a los regímenes opresivos y al bajo nivel de vida.

86

87

88

89

90

91

92

93

94

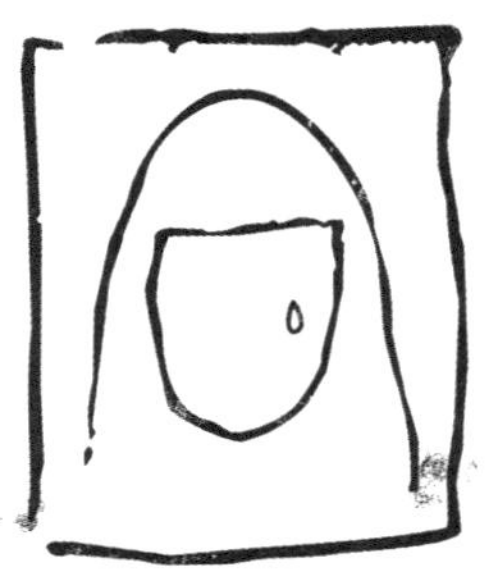

95

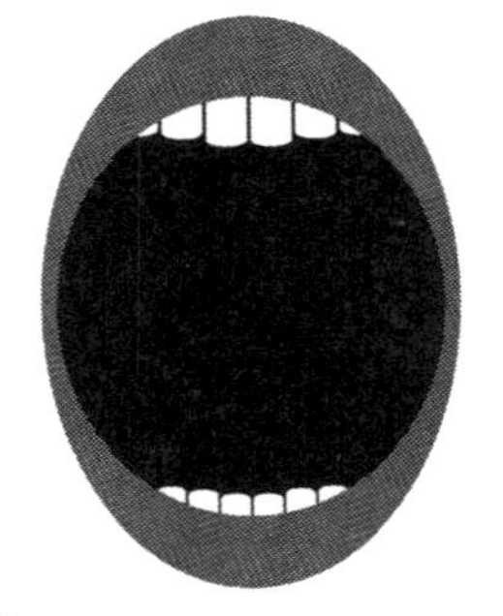

96

97

98

99

100

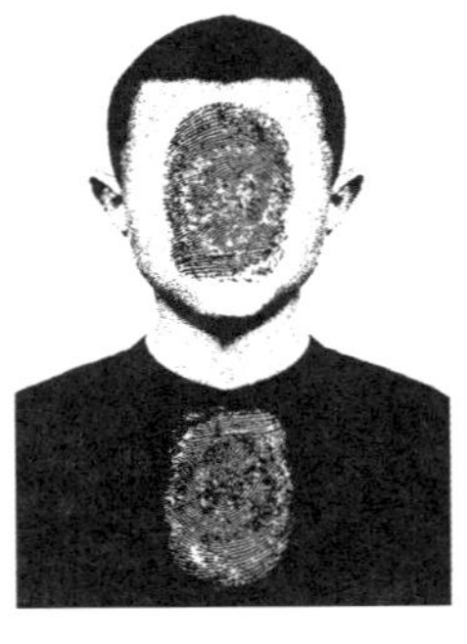

101

102

103 *

The Gag Rule / or 'On the Protection of the Security of Citizens' (2015) is a law declaring the restriction of freedoms, including expression, information, and demonstration.

La règle du bâillon / ou « sur la protection de la sécurité des citoyens » (2015) est une loi déclarant la restriction des libertés, telles que la liberté d'expression, d'information et de tenue de manifestations.

Ley mordaza / o de Protección de la Seguridad Ciudadana (2015) es una ley que declara delito o recorta libertades como la de expresión, información o manifestación.

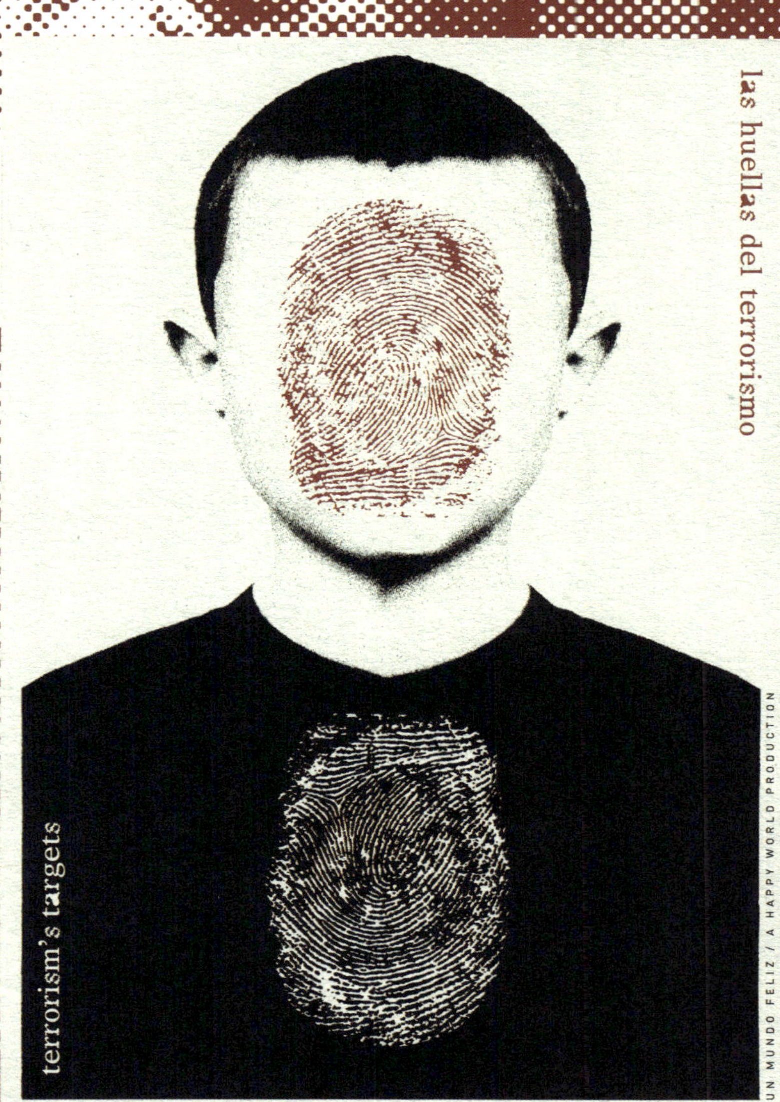

las huellas del terrorismo
terrorism's targets
UN MUNDO FELIZ / A HAPPY WORLD PRODUCTION

***If I can't dance, I don't want to be part of your revolution** / Emma Goldman replied thus to a comrade who reproached her for dancing, because it was 'inappropriate for the revolutionary cause'. Goldman was an anarchist known for her feminist suffragette writings.

***Si je ne peux pas danser, je ne veux pas prendre part à votre révolution** / c'est ainsi que répondit Emma Goldman à un camarade qui lui reprochait de danser, parce que c'était « inapproprié à la cause révolutionnaire ». Goldman était une anarchiste connue pour ses écrits féministes sur les suffragettes.

***Si no puedo bailar, tu revolución no me interesa** / respondió Emma a un compañero que le reprochaba que bailara por ser algo inapropiado para la causa revolucionaria. Emma Goldman fue una anarquista y propagandista conocida por sus escritos sufragistas feministas.

Sí

105

FREE HONG KONG
光復香港
時代革命
REVOLUTION NOW
HONG KONG

106

107 *

108

109

***Liberation theology /**
is a synthesis of Christian theology
and socio-economic analyses,
based in far-left politics – particularly
Marxism – that emphasizes 'social
concern for the poor and political
liberation for oppressed peoples.'

***La Théologie de la libération /** est
une synthèse de la théologie chrétienne
et des analyses socio-économiques,
basée sur la politique d'extrême gauche
- en particulier le marxisme - qui met
l'accent sur « la préoccupation sociale
envers les plus démunis et la libération
politique des peuples opprimés ».

***Teología de la liberación /**
es una síntesis de la teología cristiana
y de los análisis socioeconómicos,
basada en la política de la extrema
izquierda, en particular el marxismo,
que hace hincapié en «la preocupación
social por los pobres y la liberación
política de los pueblos oprimidos».

110

111

112

113

114

115

***Craftivism** / was a term coined in 2003 by Betsy Greer. Sarah Corbett and the Craftivist Collective are committed to quiet activism, using craft to change hearts, minds, and policies, and to engage people to be the positive change they wish to see in the world.

116 *

***Craftivism** / est un terme inventé en 2003 par Betsy Greer de l'association des mots anglais CRAFT (Artisanat) et ACTIVISM. Sarah Corbett et le collectif Craftivist sont engagés dans un activisme tranquille, utilisant l'artisanat pour changer les cœurs, les esprits et les politiques et pour inciter les gens à devenir le changement positif qu'ils souhaitent voir dans le monde.

117

***Craftivism** / fue acuñado en 2003 por Betsy Greer. Sarah Corbett y el Craftivist Collective están comprometidos con el activismo silencioso usando la artesanía para cambiar los corazones, las mentes, las políticas, y para comprometer a la gente a ser el cambio positivo que desean ver en el mundo.

***Guerrilla etiquette** / Robbie
Conal is known for his guerrilla poster
campaigns that combine a portrait of a
politician with a single word. The most
important rule of his 'Guerrilla Etiquette'
is 'calm, quick and (above all) polite'

***Guerrilla Etiquette** / Robbie Conal
est connu pour ses campagnes
d'affiches de guérilla qui associent le
portrait d'un politicien à un seul mot.
La règle la plus importante de sa «
Guerrilla Etiquette » est d'être Calme,
Rapide et (surtout) Poli !

***Etiqueta de guerrilla** / Robbie
Conal es conocido por sus campañas
de carteles de guerrilla que combinan
el retrato de un político con una sola
palabra. La regla más importante de
su «Guerrilla Etiquette» es ¡tranquilo,
rápido y (sobre todo) educado!

122

123

124

125

***#FeesMustFall** / was a student-led protest movement and a rallying cry for the oppressed and exploited of the world after the end of apartheid. It began in 2015 in South Africa.

***#FeesMustFall** / un mouvement de protestation mené par des étudiants, ainsi qu'un cri de ralliement pour les opprimés et les exploités du monde entier, après la fin de l'apartheid. Ce mouvement a vu le jour en Afrique du Sud en 2015.

***#FeesMustFall** / fue un movimiento de protesta liderado por estudiantes y un grito de unión para los oprimidos y explotados del mundo tras el fin del *apartheid* que comenzó en 2015 en Sudáfrica.

КАРЛ МАРКС
1818 - 2018
200-летию со дня рождения Карла Маркса
200th Anniversary of Karl Marx

132

133

134 *

135

***Carnation Revolution** / (Revolução dos Cravos), also known as the '25 April', it began as a coup organized by the Armed Forces Movement, but it was soon coupled with a popular civil resistance campaign. It started the revolutionary process that would result in a democratic Portugal.

***La Révolution des Œillets** / (Revolução dos Cravos), également surnommée le « 25 avril », a débuté par un coup d'état, organisé par un groupe de militaires, massivement soutenu par le peuple portugais, suivi d'une campagne de résistance civile. Ces événements déclenchèrent le processus révolutionnaire qui mena à la démocratisation du Portugal.

***Revolución de los Claveles** / (*Revolução dos Cravos*), también conocida como el 25 de abril, comenzó como un golpe organizado por las Fuerzas Armadas, pero pronto se unió a una campaña de resistencia civil popular revolucionaria que daría lugar a un Portugal democrático.

136

137

138

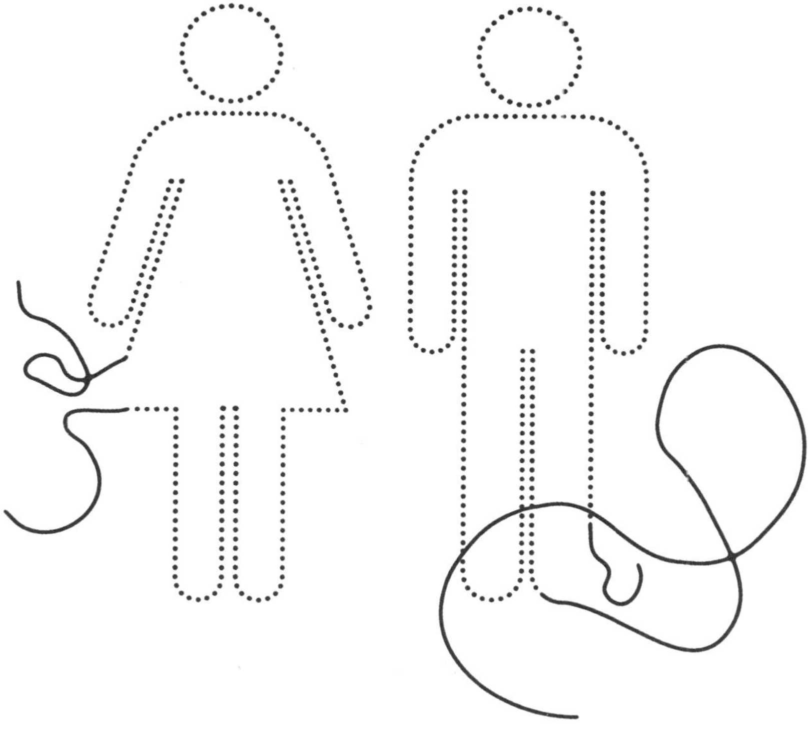

139

Guatemala has the third highest rate of femicide in the world

Between 2014 and 2016, there were 2,264 violent deaths of women in Guatemala, of which 611 were formally reported as femicide. During the same period, 59 perpetrators were imprisoned. It is a hidden problem, as a society we have to do more work in terms of information, raising awareness and training so that women recognise that they shouldn't have to suffer abuse." —Lily Wug

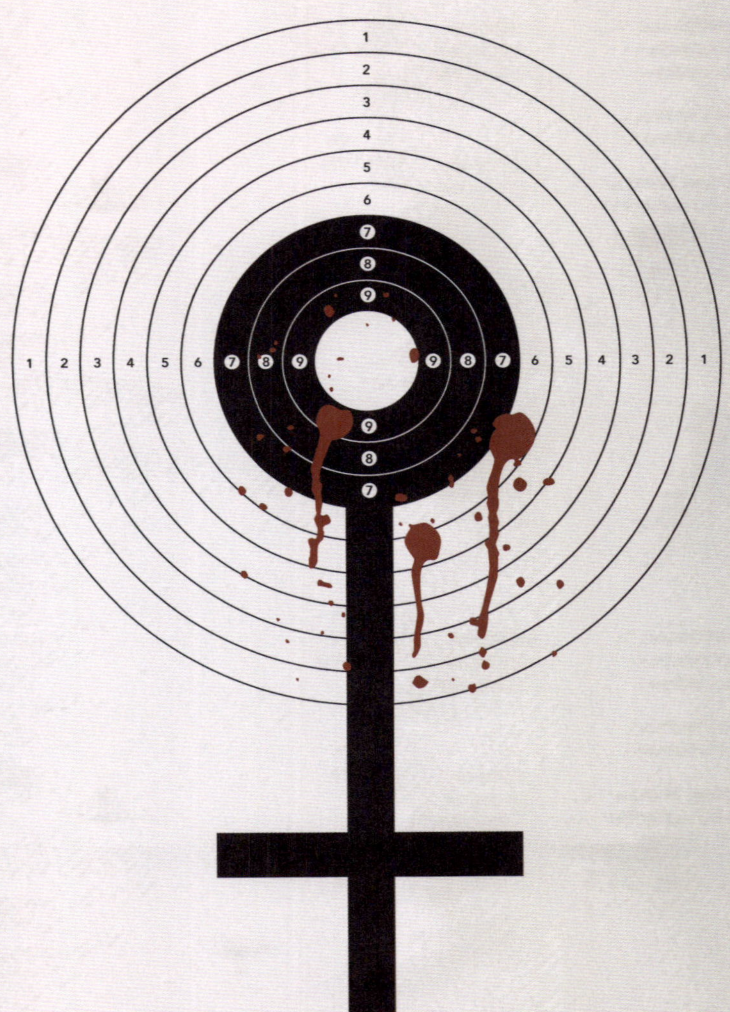

140

141

142

143

144

145

146 *

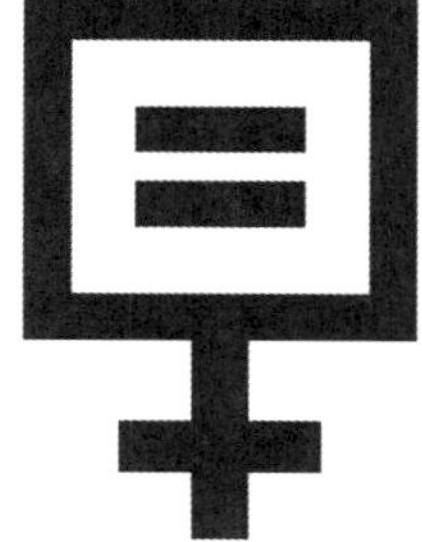

147

148

***Combahee River Collective** / was a Black feminist lesbian organization active in Boston from 1974 to 1980. They are best known for developing the Combahee River Collective Statement, a key document in the history of contemporary Black feminism.

***Collectif de la rivière Combahee** / était une organisation lesbienne féministe noire, active à Boston de 1974 à 1980. Elle est notamment connue pour sa « Déclaration du Combahee River Collective », un texte clé dans l'histoire du féminisme noir contemporain.

***Combahee River Collective** / fue una organización feminista negra y lésbica que operó en Boston entre 1974 y 1980. Es conocida por haber elaborado la Declaración Colectiva de Combahee River, un documento clave para la historia del feminismo negro contemporáneo.

149

150

151

152

153

154

155

156

157

158

159

160 *

161

***We are the power** / during the May 1968 protests in Paris, students from l'Ecole des Beaux-Arts produced more than 350 posters in the Atelier Populaire to demonstrate their demands.

***Nous sommes le pouvoir** / lors des manifestations de mai 68 à Paris, des étudiants de l'École des Beaux-Arts ont réalisé plus de 350 affiches dans l'Atelier Populaire pour exprimer leurs revendications.

***Somos el poder** / durante las protestas de mayo de 1968 en París los estudiantes de l'Ecole des Beaux-Arts produjeron más de 350 carteles en el Atelier Populaire para manifestar sus reivindicaciones.

162

163

164

165

166

167

168 *

169

170

***Girifna** / is a Sudanese non-violent resistance movement founded by university students in 2009, opposed to corruption, dictatorship, injustice, and discrimination against minorities. The word Girifna means 'we are fed up' in Arabic.

***Girifna** / est un mouvement de résistance non violent soudanais, fondé par des étudiants universitaires en 2009, s'opposant à la corruption, à la dictature, à l'injustice et à la discrimination des minorités. Le mot Girifna signifie « Nous en avons assez » en arabe.

***Girifna** / es un movimiento sudanés de resistencia no violenta fundado por estudiantes universitarios en 2009 que se opone a la corrupción, la dictadura, la injusticia y la discriminación contra las minorías. La palabra *girifna* significa «estamos hasta el gorro» en árabe.

PROTEST PICTOGRAM ACTIVISM

NI UNA
SOLA
MUJER
MUERTA
POR
ABORTO
CLANDESTINO
ABORTO LEGAL
SEGURO Y GRATUITO
CAMPAÑA NACIONAL POR EL ABORTO LEGAL, SEGURO Y GRATUITO — MARCHA DEL 8 DE MARZO DE 2018 — BUENOS AIRES, ARGENTINA

171

172 173 174

175

176

177

178

179 *

180

181

182

183

***Chicago Women's Graphics Collective** / was organized in 1970 to provide feminist posters for the growing women's liberation movement. They used silkscreen because it was inexpensive and could be produced in members' apartments.

***Chicago Women's Graphics Collective** / a été créé en 1970 pour fournir des affiches féministes au mouvement de libération des femmes en pleine expansion. Le collectif a opté pour la sérigraphie, car cette technique était peu coûteuse et pouvait être pratiquée dans les appartements de ses membres.

***Chicago Women's Graphics Collective** / se organizó en 1970 con el fin de proporcionar carteles feministas para el creciente movimiento de liberación de la mujer. Utilizaron la serigrafía porque era barata y se podía producir en los pisos de las activistas.

FIRE AND RENOVATION · THE NOTRE-DAME DE PARIS CATHEDRAL · MONDAY · APRIL 15 · 2019

184

185

186

187

188

189

190 *

191

192

***Help Spain** / in 1937, Joan Miró designed a poster that was adopted for different media, calling for support of anti-Fascist Spain during the Civil War.

***Aidez l'Espagne** / en 1937, Joan Miró créa une affiche appelant au soutien de l'Espagne antifasciste pendant la guerre civile ; cette affiche fut adoptée pour différents médias.

***Ayuda a España** / en 1937 Joan Miró diseñó un cartel que fue adoptado por diferentes medios de comunicación pidiendo apoyo para la España antifascista durante la Guerra Civil.

193 *

194

195

196

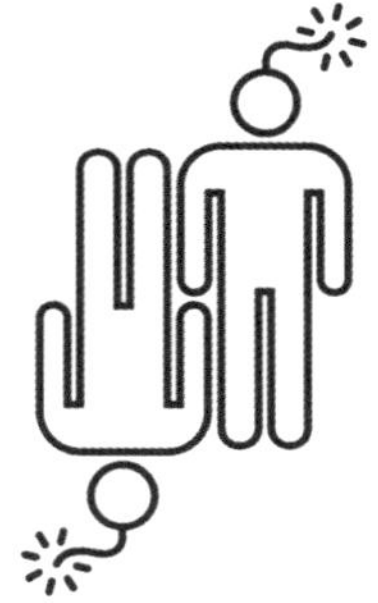

197

198

199

200

201

***El Siluetazo** / was an artistic-political practice that operated in public spaces. It was one of the emblems of the human rights movement's demand for memory, truth, and justice at the end of the last Argentine dictatorship in 1983.

***El Siluetazo** / un mouvement argentin intervenant dans l'espace public par des performances artistiques à portée politique. C'était l'un des emblèmes des revendications de mémoire, de vérité et de justice du mouvement des droits de l'homme, à la fin de la dernière dictature argentine en 1983.

***El Siluetazo** / fue una práctica artístico-política desarrollada en el espacio público y uno de los emblemas de la reivindicación de la memoria, la verdad y la justicia por parte del movimiento de derechos humanos a finales de la última dictadura argentina en 1983.

PROTEST PICTOGRAM ACTIVISM

202

203

204

205

206

207

208

209

210

211

212

213

214 *

***Artists Against Police Violence** /
is an online space featuring
graphics and artwork to be used
for communities against police
murders of Black people.

***Artists Against Police Violence** /
(Artistes contre la violence policière)
est un espace en ligne présentant des
dessins et des œuvres d'art destinés à
être utilisés par les communautés contre
les meurtres de Noirs par la police.

***Artists Against Police Violence** /
es una plataforma con diseños y
obras de arte para ser utilizados por
la comunidad contra los abusos y
los asesinatos policiales de personas
negras.

PROTEST PICTOGRAM ACTIVISM

#blackLivesMatter
BLACK
LIVES
MATTER

216

***Pussy Galore** / in 1994, Women's Design Research Unit (WD+RU) created an experimental typeface for FUSE 12 with the language used by, for, and against women.

217

***Pussy Galore** / en 1994, la Women's Design Research Unit (WD+RU) crée pour FUSE 12 une police de caractères expérimentale avec le langage utilisé par, pour et contre les femmes.

218

***Pussy Galore** / en 1994 Women's Design Research Unit (WD+RU) crea para FUSE 12 un tipo de letra experimental con el lenguaje utilizado por, para y contra las mujeres.

219

220

221

222

223

224

225

226

227

228

229

230

231

232

233

234

235

236

237 *

238

***The March for Our Lives** / (MFOL) was a student-led demonstration in support of legislation to prevent gun violence in the United States, inresponse to the Stoneman Douglas High School shooting.

239

***Marche pour nos vies** / (MFOL) était une manifestation menée par des étudiants en faveur d'une législation visant à prévenir la violence armée aux États-Unis, en réaction à la fusillade du lycée Stoneman Douglas.

240

***La Marcha por Nuestras Vidas** / (MFOL) fue una manifestación liderada por estudiantes en apoyo de la legislación para prevenir la violencia con armas de fuego en los Estados Unidos y en respuesta al tiroteo en la escuela secundaria Stoneman Douglas.

241 *

242

***March for Peace** / in 1962, Satish Kumar and his friend, E. P. Menon, inspired by Bertrand Russell's civil disobedience against the atomic bomb, decided to march from India to the four nuclear-armed capitals: Moscow, Paris, London, and Washington.

***Marche pour la paix** / en 1962, Satish Kumar et son ami E. P. Menon, inspirés par la désobéissance civile de Bertrand Russell contre la bombe atomique, décident de marcher de l'Inde vers les quatre capitales nucléaires : Moscou, Paris, Londres et Washington.

***Marcha por la Paz** / en 1962 Satish Kumar y su amigo E. P. Menon, inspirados por la desobediencia civil contra la bomba atómica de Bertrand Russell, decidieron realizar una marcha desde la India a las cuatro capitales con armas nucleares: Moscú, París, Londres y Washington.

PROTEST PICTOGRAM ACTIVISM

243

244

INCARCERATION IS NOT AN EQUAL OPPORTUNITY PUNISHMENT / EL ENCARCELAMIENTO ES UN CASTIGO QUE PROMUEVE LA DESIGUALDAD
www.prisonsticks.com

245

246

***Marcha Migrante** / Border Angels organizes caravans that meet with community groups to support them in their struggles and to educate people about migrant deaths. The sixth Marcha was called the 'Trail of Tears', because it covered territory where migrants have perished.

***Marcha Migrante** / l'organisation Border Angels (Anges des frontières) organise des caravanes qui rencontrent des groupes communautaires pour les soutenir dans leurs luttes et pour informer les gens sur les décès de migrants. La sixième Marche a été appelée « Piste des larmes », car elle parcourait un territoire où des migrants ont péri.

***Marcha Migrante** / Border Angels organiza caravanas que se reúnen con grupos comunitarios para apoyarlos en sus luchas y para educar sobre las muertes de los migrantes. La sexta Marcha fue llamada «Sendero de Lágrimas» porque cubría el territorio donde los migrantes habían perecido.

247

248

249

250

251

252

253

254

255

***Ni una menos** / is a fourth-wave grassroots feminist movement in Argentina that campaigns on the issues of gender-based violence, gender roles, sexual harassment, gender pay gap, sexual objectification, legality of abortion, sex workers' rights, and transgender rights.

***Ni una menos** / (Pas une de moins) est un mouvement féministe communautaire argentin dont la quatrième vague fait des campagnes contre la violence sexiste, les rôles de genre, le harcèlement sexuel, l'écart salarial entre les sexes, l'objectivation sexuelle et en faveur de la légalisation de l'avortement, des droits des travailleurs du sexe et des transgenres.

***Ni una menos** / es un movimiento feminista argentino de base (de cuarta ola) que hace campaña contra la violencia de género, los roles de género, el acoso sexual, la brecha salarial entre los géneros, la cosificación sexual, el aborto, y los derechos de las trabajadoras sexuales y los transexuales.

***Women's rights activists /**
Stella Browne (1880–1955) was a
feminist and birth control campaigner.
She was one of the primary women in
the fight for women's right to control
and make decisions regarding their
sexual choices.

***Militante des droits de la femme /**
Stella Browne (1880-1955) était une
militante féministe et pionnière du
contrôle des naissances. Elle a été
l'une des premières femmes à se
battre pour le droit des femmes et à
défendre la liberté totale dans leurs
choix sexuels.

***Activista por los derechos de
la mujer /** Stella Browne (1880-1955)
fue una feminista defensora del
control de la natalidad y una de
las principales luchadoras por el
derecho de las mujeres a controlar
y tomar decisiones en relación
con sus opciones sexuales.

263

264

265

266

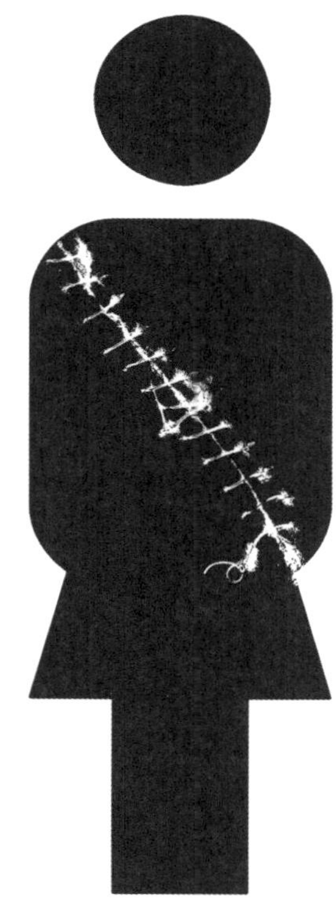

268

267

269 *

***No More Miss America!** / was a
feminist demonstration held at the Miss
America 1968 contest, organized by
New York Radical Women. They tossed
symbolic feminine products, including
bras, makeup, and other items,
into a 'Freedom Trash Can'.

***No More Miss America!** / (Plus de Miss
Amérique !) fut une manifestation féministe
contre le concours de beauté de Miss
Amérique en 1968, organisée par le groupe
« New York Radical Women ». Ces femmes
ont jeté des objets féminins symboliques,
notamment des soutiens-gorge, des
produits de maquillage et d'autres articles,
dans une « Poubelle de la Liberté ».

***¡No Más Miss América!** / fue una
protesta feminista celebrada durante
el concurso Miss América 1968,
organizada por las Mujeres Radicales
de Nueva York, en la que se arrojaron
productos femeninos simbólicos, como
sostenes, maquillaje y otros artículos,
a un «cubo de basura de la libertad».

PROTEST PICTOGRAM ACTIVISM

270 *

***I am an optical illusion**
—Clotilde (Top model)

***Je suis une illusion d'optique**
—Clotilde (Top model)

***Soy una ilusión óptica**
—Clotilde (Top model)

271

272

273

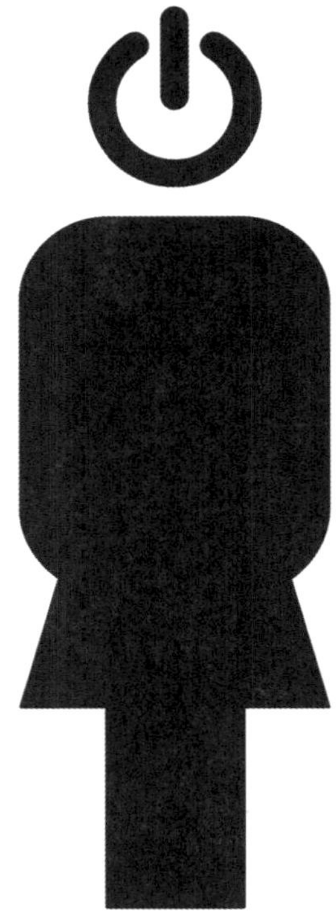

275

274

276

277

279 *

280

281

282

***Body-poster** / FEMEN is an international women's movement of brave, topless, female activists, who paint themselves with slogans and crown their heads with flowers. / Sextremism is a nonviolent but highly aggressive form of provocation against patriarchy.

***Corps - affiche** / FEMEN est un mouvement international de femmes militantes courageuses qui organisent des actions, essentiellement seins nus, des slogans peints sur le corps et la tête couronnée de fleurs. / Leur féminisme radical, le sextremisme, est une forme de provocation non violente, mais très agressive envers le patriarcat.

***Cuerpo-cartel** / FEMEN es un movimiento internacional de mujeres activistas valientes en *topless*, pintadas con lemas y coronadas con flores. / El *sextremismo* es una forma no violenta pero altamente agresiva de provocación contra el patriarcado.

283

284

285

286 *

287

288

289

290

291

***See Red Women's Workshop** /
was founded by three ex-art students
in 1974. It was a women's collective
interested in examining and combatting
the negative images of women
in advertising and the media.

***See Red Women's Workshop** /
a été fondé en 1974 par trois anciennes
étudiantes en art. C'était un collectif
de femmes qui se réunissaient pour
examiner et combattre les images
négatives de la femme dans la publicité
et les médias.

***See Red Women's Workshop** /
fue fundado por tres exalumnas de
arte en 1974, un colectivo constituido
por mujeres interesadas en agruparse
para detectar y combatir las imágenes
negativas de la mujer en la publicidad
y los medios de comunicación.

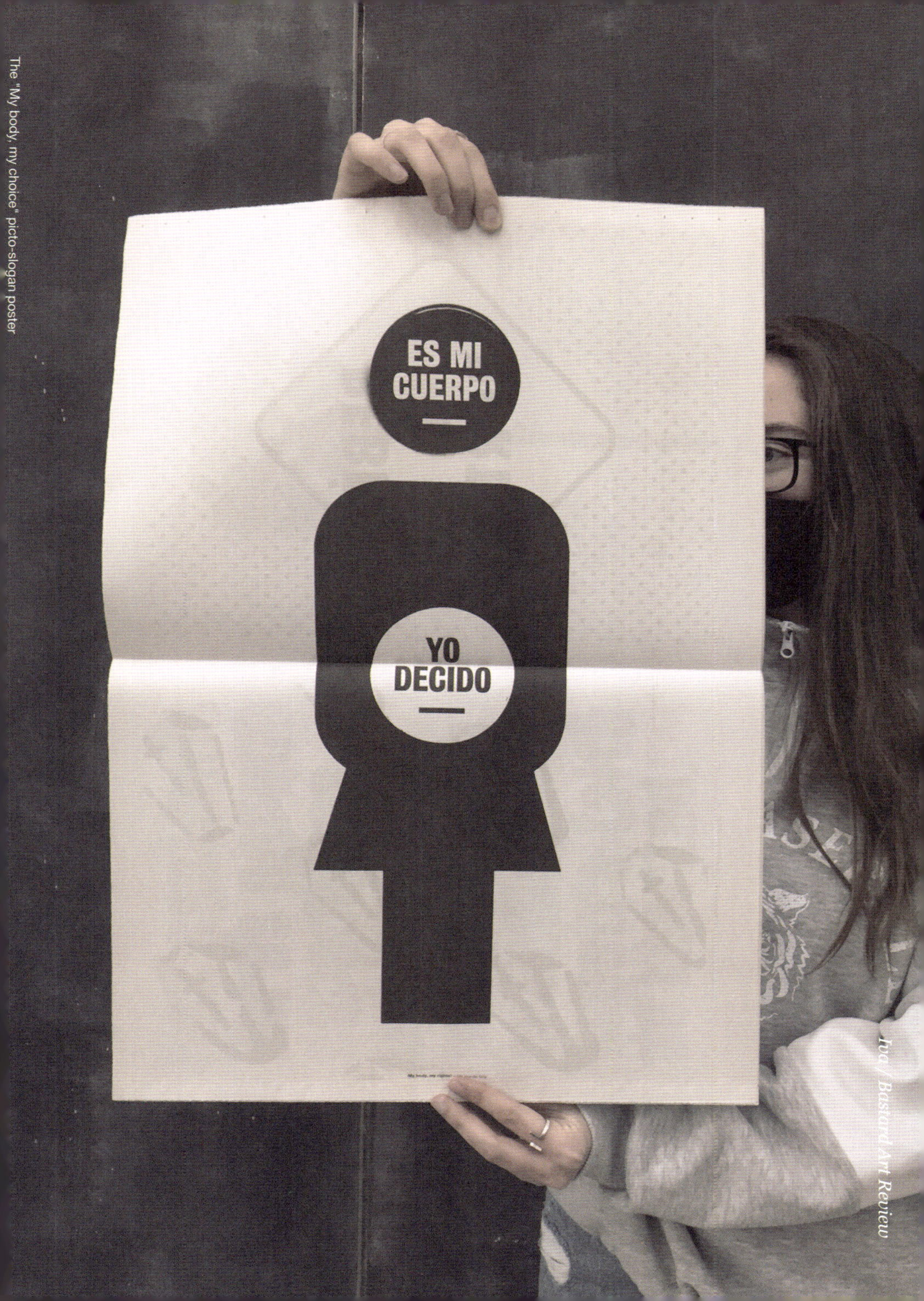

ES MI
CUERPO

YO
DECIDO

292

293

294

295

296

297 *

298

299

***Movimento delle Sardine** /
the Sardines movement organized
an ongoing series of peaceful
demonstrations to protest against the
right-wing surge in Italy and against
the political rhetoric of right-wing
leader Matteo Salvini.

***Movimento delle Sardine** /
le mouvement des Sardines a organisé
une série de manifestations pacifiques
pour protester contre le populisme
et contre la montée de l'extrême droite
en Italie, représentée par son leader
de la Ligue du Nord, Matteo Salvini.

***Movimento delle Sardine** /
el movimiento de las Sardinas organizó
una serie de manifestaciones pacíficas
para protestar contra el avance de la
extrema derecha en Italia y contra la
retórica política del líder de la derecha
Matteo Salvini.

300

301

302

303

304

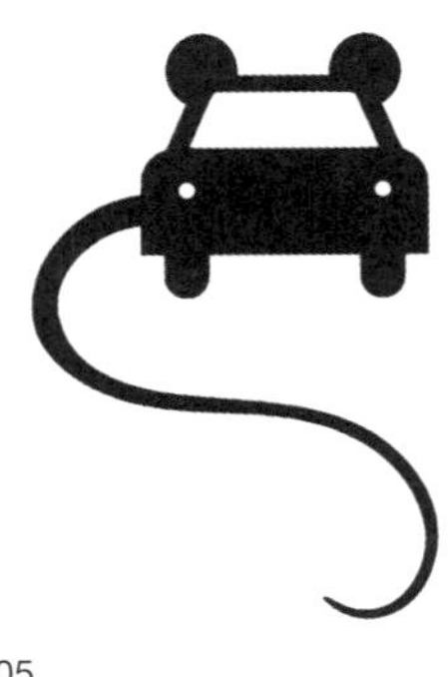

305

306

307

308

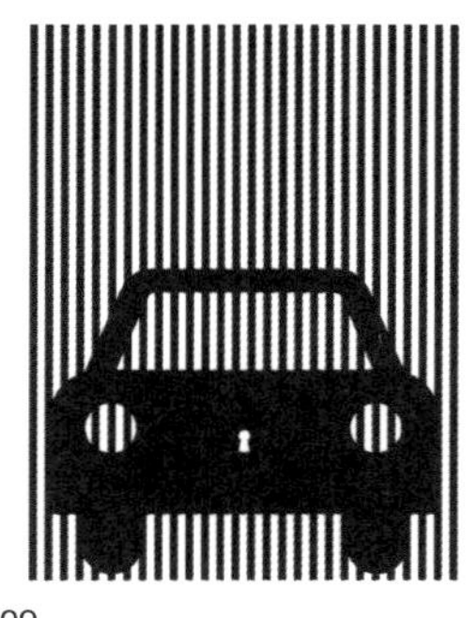

309

310

311

312

313

314 *

315

316

317

***Reclaim the Streets** / (RTS)
is a collective with a shared ideal
of community ownership of public
spaces and opposition to automobiles.
RTS stages non-violent, direct action
street-reclaiming events, such as the
'invasion' of a major road or freeway
to stage a party.

***Reclaim the Streets** / RTS) est
un collectif qui partage l'idéal de la
propriété communautaire des espaces
publics et est opposé à la voiture.
RTS organise des actions directes
non violentes de récupération des rues,
telles que l' « invasion » d'une route
principale ou d'une autoroute pour
organiser une fête.

***Reclaim the Streets** / (RTS) es un
colectivo con un ideal compartido de
propiedad comunitaria de los espacios
públicos y opuesto al coche. RTS
escenifica eventos de acción directa
no violenta para reclamar la calle como
la *invasión* de una carretera o autovía
principal para organizar una fiesta.

An end in terror is preferable to terror without end. —Sophie Scholl

a Greek word meaning "many" and tics meaning "bloodsucking creatures". —Robin Williams

318

319 *

320

321

322

323

324

325

326

***Unfair play** / the pictograms designed for the 1972 Munich Olympics by Otl Aicher, Gerhard Joksch and Dept. XI team were a triumph of the rationalist functionalism mode. / **Olympukes** (olympics + puke), by Jonathan Barnbrook, reflect the deception, manipulation, and greed endemic to the games.

***Jeu déloyal** / les pictogrammes conçus par Otl Aicher pour les Jeux Olympiques de Munich en 1972 célébraient le rationalisme et la fonctionnalisme. / La police de caractères **Olympukes** (ce qui pourrait être traduit par « Olymgerbe ») créée par Jonathan Barnbrook reflète la supercherie, la manipulation et l'avidité endémiques des jeux.

***Juego sucio** / los pictogramas de los Juegos Olímpicos de Múnich de 1972 diseñados por Otl Aicher, Gerhard Joksch y el Dept. XI fueron el triunfo del espíritu funcionalista racionalista. / **Olympukes** (olimpíadas + vómito) de Jonathan Barnbrook reflejan el engaño, la manipulación y la codicia endémica de los juegos.

PROTEST PICTOGRAM ACTIVISM

327

328

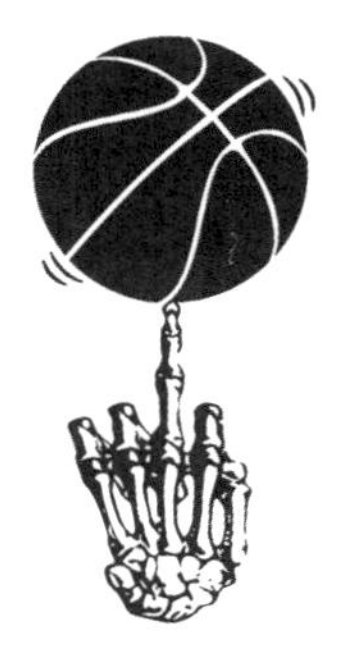

329

330

***Umbrella Revolution /**
was a political movement that emerged during the Hong Kong democracy protests of 2014. Its name arose from the use of umbrellas as a tool for passive resistance against the use of pepper spray by the Hong Kong police to disperse the crowds.

***La Révolution des Parapluies /**
est un mouvement politique qui vu le jour lors des manifestations pour la démocratie à Hong Kong en 2014. Son nom vient de l'utilisation de parapluies comme moyen de résistance passive par les manifestants contre l'utilisation de gaz poivré par la police.

***La Revolución de los Paraguas /**
fue un movimiento surgido a raíz de las manifestaciones por la democracia de Hong Kong en 2014. Su nombre procede del uso de paraguas como útiles de resistencia pasiva frente al empleo de gas pimienta por la policía para dispersar a los manifestantes.

333 *

334

335

336

337

338

339 *

340

341

***The Smiley** / in 1963, Harvey Ball created the most famous symbol of happiness, a simple yellow smiling face that was accompanied by the legend, 'Have a nice day'. / **The Smiling Sun** was designed in 1975 by Anne Lund. It is the international symbol of the anti-nuclear movement.

***Smiley** / en 1963, Harvey Ball créa le plus célèbre symbole de bonheur, le rond jaune figurant un visage souriant, accompagné de la légende : « Have a nice day » (Bonne journée). / Le **Soleil souriant** fut inventé en 1975 par Anne Lund et est devenu le symbole international du mouvement antinucléaire.

***El Smiley** / en 1963 Harvey Ball creó el símbolo más famoso de la felicidad, una simple cara sonriente amarilla que iba acompañada de la leyenda: «Que tengas un buen día». / **El Sol Sonriente** fue diseñado en 1975 por la activista danesa Anne Lund y es el símbolo internacional del movimiento antinuclear.

342

343

344

345

346

347

348

349

350

351 *

354

352

353

356

357

355

358

***Snow Revolution** / the name given to protests against the results of the 2011 Russian legislative elections. Response: a law allowing censorship of websites and online content that has led to the closure of the country's main independent digital media.

***La Révolution blanche ou Révolution des neiges** / désigne la contestation des élections législatives russes de 2011. Réponse : une loi autorisant la censure des sites web et des contenus en ligne qui a entraîné la fermeture des principaux médias numériques indépendants du pays.

***Snow Revolution** / son las protestas contra los resultados de las elecciones legislativas rusas de 2011. Respuesta: una ley que permite la censura de webs y contenidos en línea y que ha llevado al cierre de los principales medios digitales independientes del país.

'SHUT UP! THE VOICE OF DEMOCRACY IN DANGER' IS A REACTION TO THE SHOCKING DEATH OF SLOVAK JOURNALIST JAN KUCIAK AND HIS FIANCÉE, MARTINA KUSHNIHOVA, IN FEB. 2018. AS A REPORTER, KUCIAK FOCUSED MAINLY ON INVESTIGATING TAX FRAUD INVOLVING SEVERAL BUSINESSMEN WITH CONNECTION TO TOP-LEVEL SLOVAK POLITICIANS

360

***Yayoflautas** / a term used for retirees protesting in defense of public pensions in Spain. It is derived from 'Los yayos', a term of endearment for grandparents, and 'perroflauta', a derogatory term for the 'Indignados' of the 15-M movement.

361

***Yayoflautas** / terme désignant les manifestants retraités du mouvement de contestation, descendus dans la rue pour défendre les pensions publiques en Espagne. « Los iaios » est le nom affectueux donné aux grands-parents, tandis que les « indignés » étaient péjorativement appelés « perroflautas » pendant le 15-M.

362 *

***Yayoflautas** / término que designa a los jubilados que se manifiestan en defensa de las pensiones públicas en España. *Yayos* es un apelativo cariñoso dado a los abuelos. Durante el 15-M a los *indignados* se les llamó despectivamente «perroflautas».

363

364

365

366

We need to get angry and understand what is at stake. And then we need to transform that anger into action and so stand together united and just

367

368

369

370

371

372 *

***Amazon** / Raoni Metuktire is an environmentalist leader. He is a chief of the Kayapo people, a Brazilian Indigenous group. Raoni is a living symbol of the fight for the preservation of both the Amazon rainforest and indigenous culture.

***Amazonie** / Raoni Metuktire est un leader écologiste. C'est un des grands chefs du peuple Kayapo, un groupe indigène brésilien, et un symbole vivant de la lutte pour la préservation de la forêt amazonienne et de la culture indigène.

***La Amazonia** / Raoni Metuktire es un líder ambientalista y el jefe del pueblo Kayapo, un grupo indígena brasileño. Raoni es un símbolo viviente de la lucha por la preservación de la selva amazónica y la cultura indígena.

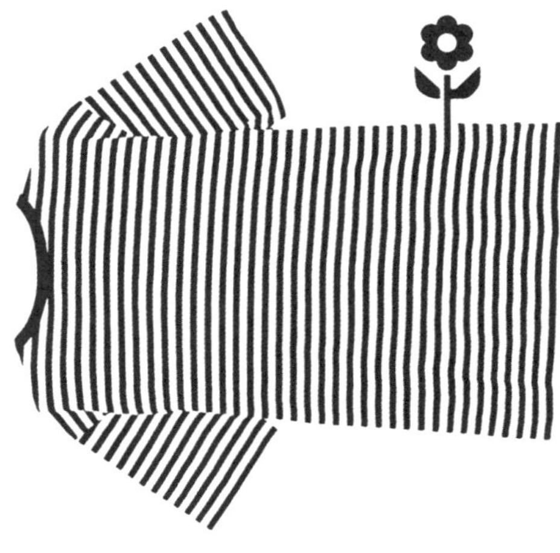

373

374

375 *

376

377

378

***The Graphic Workshop** /
was started by students at The
Massachusetts College of Art and
Design as a "visual propaganda unit".
They produced posters between
1970 and 1992 criticizing war, racism,
and environmental destruction.

***The Graphic Workshop** / a été lancé
par des étudiants du Massachusetts
College of Art and Design comme une
« unité de propagande visuelle ». Ils ont
produit des affiches entre 1970 et 1992
critiquant la guerre, le racisme et
la destruction de l'environnement.

***The Graphic Workshop** / fue iniciado
por los estudiantes del Massachusetts
College of Art and Design como
una «unidad de propaganda visual».
Produjeron carteles entre 1970 y 1992
criticando la guerra, el racismo y
la destrucción del medio ambiente.

THERE IS A STATE OF EMERGENCY AND
NATURAL DISASTER SITUATION IN IRAN

THE GOLESTAN FLOODS / 19 MARCH 2019

379

380 *

381

382

383

384

385

386

387

***The God Bless Graffiti Coalition /** was founded in Chicago to combat growing national and international anti-graffiti trends. In 2002, GBGC published a brochure, 'Give Graffiti the Thumbs Up', to help educate the public on the truth about graffiti.

***The God Bless Graffiti Coalition /** a été fondée à Chicago pour lutter contre les tendances nationales et internationales croissantes anti-graffiti. En 2002, GBGC a publié une brochure intitulée « Give Graffiti the Thumbs Up » (Donnez un coup de pouce aux graffitis), afin de sensibiliser le public sur cette forme d'expression artistique.

***The God Bless Graffiti Coalition /** fue fundada en Chicago para combatir las crecientes tendencias antigrafiti nacionales e internacionales. En 2002 GBGC publicó el folleto «Give Graffiti the Thumbs Up» para educar al público sobre la verdad del grafiti.

388

389

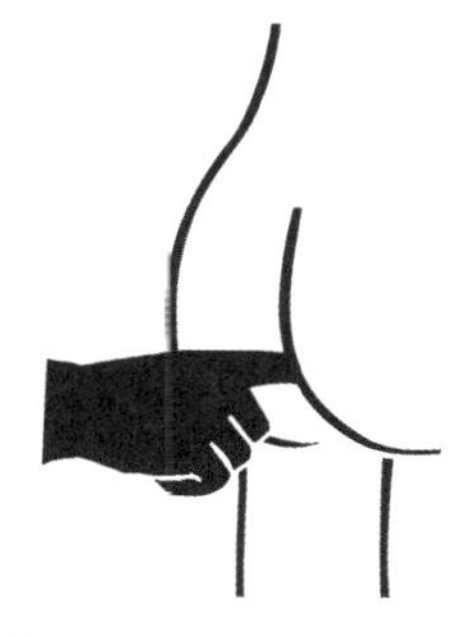

390

391

392

393

394

395

396

397

398

399

400

401

402

403 *

404

405

***15-M** / a movement of the 'Indignados', who camped in squares throughout Spain with the intention of promoting a more participatory democracy and limiting the dominance of banks and corporations. It has influenced movements such as the Occupy movement, YoSoy1328, and Nuit debout.

***15-M** / un mouvement des « Indignados », (Indignés) occupant les places de toute l'Espagne avec l'intention de promouvoir une démocratie plus participative et de limiter la domination des banques et des entreprises. Il a influencé des mouvements tels que le mouvement Occupy, YoSoy1328 et Nuit debout.

***15-M** / o movimiento de los indignados, acampó en plazas de toda España con la intención de promover una democracia más participativa y limitar el dominio de bancos y corporaciones. Ha tenido influencia en otros movimientos como Occupy, YoSoy1328 o Nuit debout.

406 *

Voces con Futura /
the graphic voice of the 15-M movement.
(see pages 36-37)

Voces con Futura /
la voix graphique du 15-M.
(voir pages 36 - 37)

Voces con Futura /
la voz gráfica de 15-M.
(ver páginas 36-37)

THIS IS MY BODY
MY DRESS DOESN'T MEAN YES
THE STATE OF MY VAGINA IS NONE OF YOUR BUSINESS
WOMEN DECLARE WAR ON RAPE
FLIRTING IS NOT CONSENT SILENCE IS NOT CONSENT

You cannot buy the revolution. You cannot make the revolution. You can only be the revolution. It is in your spirit, or it is nowhere. —Ursula K. Le Guin

Vous ne pouvez pas acheter la Révolution. Vous ne pouvez pas faire la Révolution. Vous pouvez seulement être la Révolution. Elle est dans votre esprit, ou bien elle n'est nulle part. —Ursula K. Le Guin

No puedes comprar la revolución. No puedes hacer la revolución. Sólo puedes ser la revolución. Está en tu espíritu, o no está en ninguna parte. —Ursula K. Le Guin

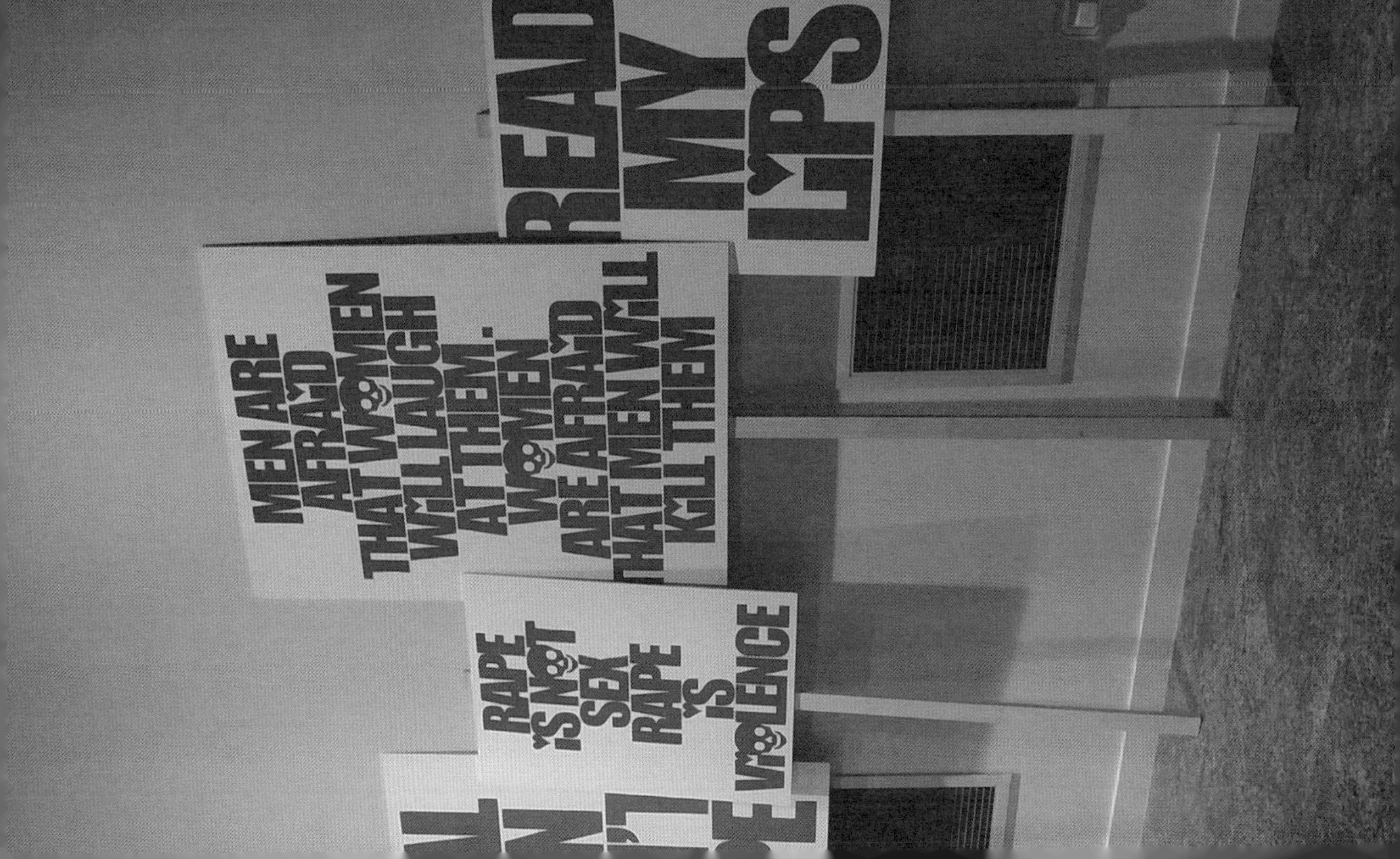

407

408

409

410 *

411

412

413

414

415

***Gran Fury** / from 1987 to 1995, this AIDS activist art collective created bold messages like 'Kissing Doesn't Kill', 'Welcome to America', 'Women Don't Get AIDS', and 'Men use Condoms', as well as the postcards of the 'Read My Lips' series.

***Gran Fury** / de 1987 à 1995, ce collectif artistique militant contre le sida a créé des messages courageux et tranchants, tels que « Embrasser ne tue pas », « Bienvenue en Amérique », « Les femmes n'attrapent pas le sida » et « Mecs, mettez des capotes », ainsi que les cartes postales de la série « Lis sur mes lèvres ».

***Gran Fury** / de 1987 a 1995 el colectivo artístico activista del SIDA creó mensajes audaces como «Besar no mata», «Bienvenido a América», «Las mujeres no contraen el SIDA», «Los hombres usan condones» y tarjetas postales como las de la serie «Lee mis labios».

DON'T
HIDE
SPEAK
OUT

416

417 *

***Anti-austerity activists** / known
as the Indignant Citizens Movement,
it involved demonstrations and strikes
against plans to cut public spending
and raise taxes in Greece.

418

***Le Mouvement anti-austérité
en Grèce** / connu sous le nom de
« Mouvement des citoyens indignés »
a organisé des manifestations et des
grèves pour marquer son opposition à
la réduction des dépenses publiques
et à la hausse des impôts et des taxes.

419

***Activistas contra la austeridad** /
conocidos como el Movimiento
de Ciudadanos Indignados, en Grecia
participaron en manifestaciones y
huelgas provocadas por los planes
de recorte del gasto público
y el aumento de los impuestos.

420

421   422   423

424 *

425

426

427

Fast Food Nation / by Eric Schlosser examines the local and global influence of the United States fast food industry. / **Super Size Me**, by Morgan Spurlock, documents a 30-day period during which he ate only McDonald's food.

Fast Food Nation / (Le pays de la restauration rapide) le livre d'Eric Schlosser étudie l'impact local et mondial de l'industrie américaine de la restauration rapide. / **Super Size Me** (ou la Malbouffe à l'américaine), un film documentaire de Morgan Spurlock, qui le représente se nourrissant exclusivement chez McDonald's pendant un mois.

Fast Food Nation / de Eric Schlosser, examina la influencia local y mundial de la industria de la comida rápida de los Estados Unidos. / **Super Size Me** de Morgan Spurlock, documenta un período de 30 días durante el cual sólo comió comida de McDonald's.

428

429

430

431

432 *

433

434

435

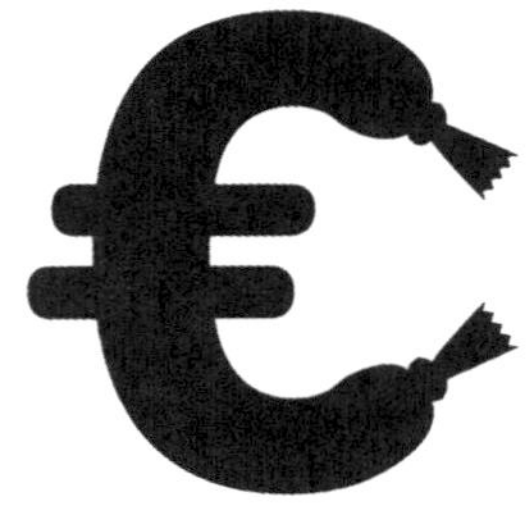

436

***Dirty Protest** / in 1978, some prisoners of the IRA and INLA refused to leave their cells to shower or use the lavatory because of attacks by prison officers. They also began smearing excrement on the walls of their cells.

***Dirty Protest** / (la protestation par la saleté) en 1978, des prisonniers de l'IRA et de l'INLA ont refusé de quitter leur cellule pour prendre une douche ou utiliser les toilettes pour protester contre les attaques des agents pénitentiaires. Ils ont également étalé des excréments sur les murs de leurs cellules.

***Protesta Sucia** / en 1978 algunos prisioneros del IRA e INLA se negaron a salir de sus celdas para ducharse o usar el baño debido a los ataques de los oficiales de la prisión [...] y acabaron untando con excrementos las paredes de sus celdas.

MURDER, HONOR, AND FREEDOM OF THE PRESS — DEADLY CENSORSHIP

ONE WAY
A society that puts equality before freedom will get neither. A society that puts freedom before equality will get a high degree of both. —Milton Friedman

437

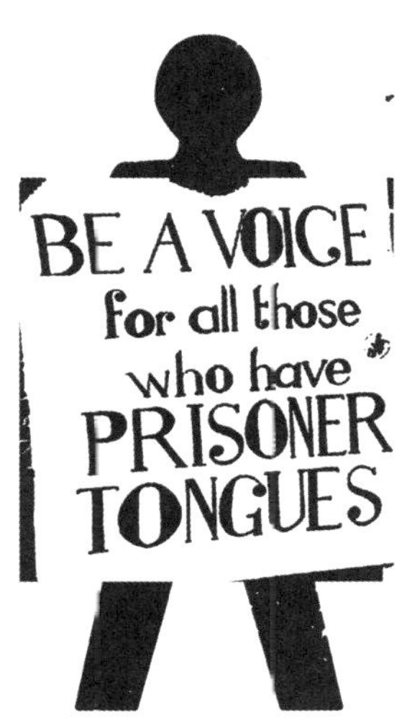

438

439

440 *

***Motherfuckers** / Up Against the Wall Motherfucker was an anarchist affinity group based in New York City. This 'street gang with analysis' was famous for its direct action and for inspiring members of the Weather Underground and the Yippies. Their name came from a poem by Amiri Baraka.

***Motherfuckers** / Up Against the Wall Motherfucker était un groupe d'anarchistes basé à New York. Ce « gang de rue avec de l'analyse » était connu pour ses actions directes et pour avoir inspiré les membres du Weather Underground et des Yippies. Leur nom vient d'un poème d'Amiri Baraka.

***Motherfuckers** / Up Against the Wall Motherfucker fue un grupo de afinidad anarquista con sede en Nueva York. Esta «pandilla callejera con análisis» es famosa por utilizar la acción directa e inspirar a miembros del Weather Underground y los *yippies*. Su nombre proviene de un poema de Amiri Baraka.

441 *

442

443

444

***Safety pin** / this tiny symbol become a token of support against hate, racism, sexism, and violence in the wake of Donald Trump's election as US president. #illridewithyou in Sydney, #safetypin in Britain, and #SafetyPin in the US.

***Safety pin** / l'épingle de sûreté, ce minuscule objet est devenu le signe de solidarité et de soutien aux minorités aux États-Unis contre la haine, le racisme, le sexisme et la violence - #illridewithyou à Sydney, #safetypin en Grande-Bretagne ou #SafetyPin aux États-Unis depuis l'élection de Donald Trump à la présidence.

***Alfiler** / este pequeño símbolo se ha convertido en una muestra de apoyo contra el odio, el racismo, el sexismo y la violencia: #illridewithyou en Sidney, #safetypin de Gran Bretaña o #SafetyPin en los EE.UU. tras la victoria electoral de Donald Trump.

PROTEST PICTOGRAM ACTIVISM

ACT NOW TO DEFEND HUMAN RIGHTS IN WESTERN SAHARA
FREE SAHARA

CRIMEA / UKRAINE 2014

LIFE

I hold it that a little rebellion now and then is a good thing, and as necessary in the political world as storms in the physical. —Thomas Jefferson

We won't have a society if we destroy the environment. —Margaret Mead

The activist is not the man who says the river is dirty. The activist is the man who cleans up the river. —Ross Perot

Home is the most dangerous place for women
25 November, the International Day for the Elimination of Violence against Women

I am not free while any woman is unfree, even when her shackles are very different from my own. —Audre Lorde

indignáos!
#spanishrevolution

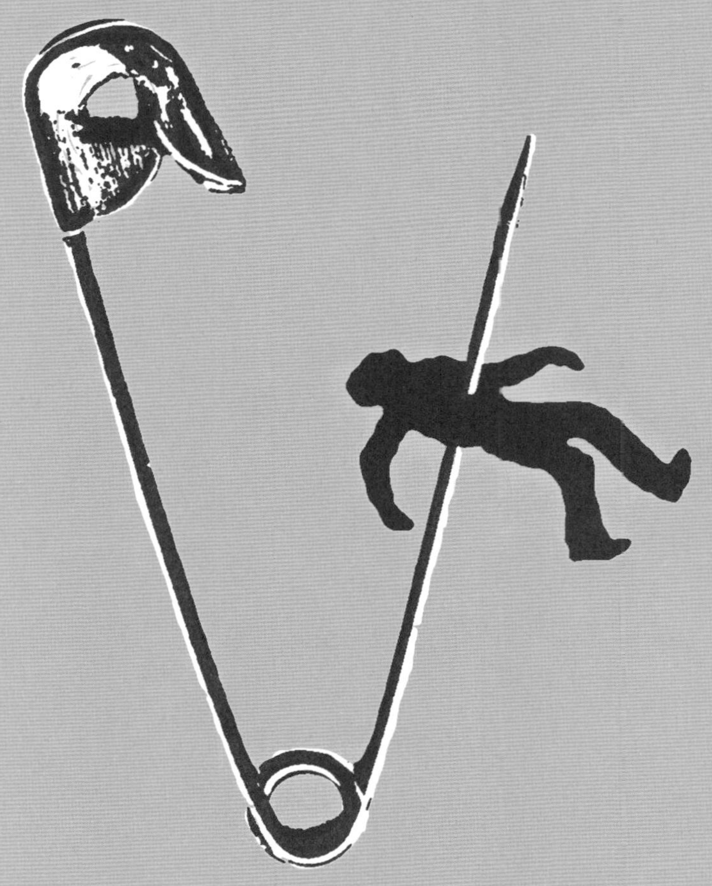

People shouldn't be afraid of their government. Governments should be afraid of their people. —Alan Moore, V for Vendetta

I do not want art for a few; any more than education for a few; or freedom for a few... —William Morris

EDUCATION IS LIKE LIBERTY IT ISN'T GIVEN IT'S TAKEN

STOP DESAHUCIOS — STOP EVICTIONS
VIVIENDA PARA LA GENTE NO PARA EL LUCRO!
HOUSING FOR PEOPLE NOT FOR PROFITS!
DE WOHNUNGEN FÜR MENSCHEN, LEICHT HABITANTS(ES), POEN PROFIT!
LE HUIZEN VOOR MENSEN, NIET VOOR WINST!
ROMANIA DLA TYLKO! THE PLATFORM OF PLATAFORMA CITIZENS AFECTADOS AFFECTED POR BY HIPOTECA MORTGAGES (PAH)
ACTION ACCIÓN FOR POR HOUSING DERECHO RIGHTS A LA VIVIENDA
Activism begins with you. Democracy begins with you; get out there, get active! Tag; you're it. —Thom Hartmann

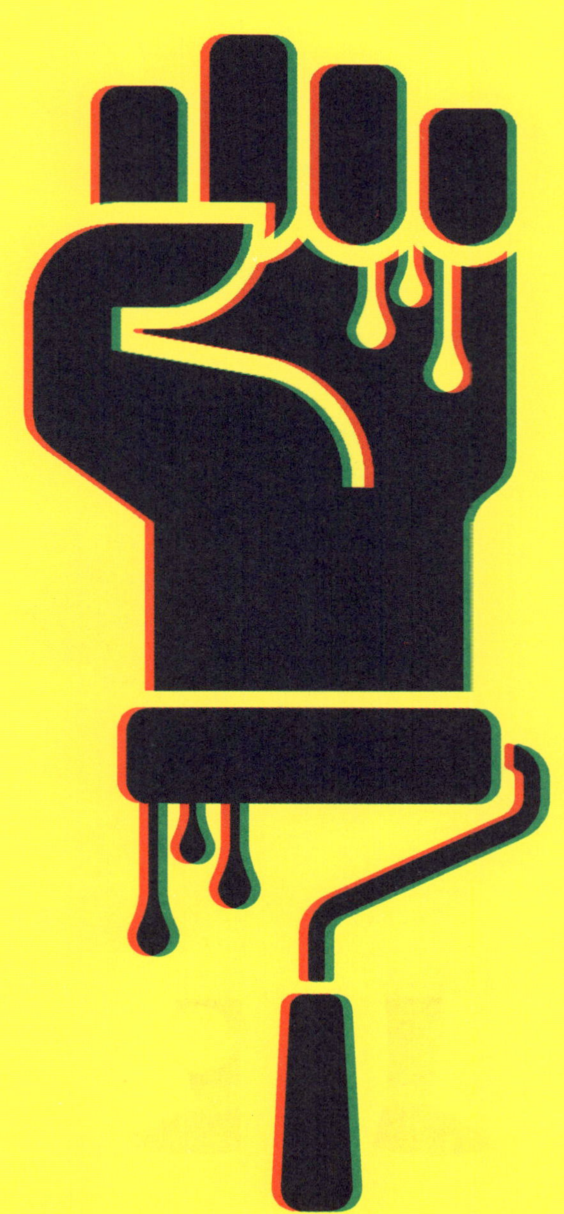

Protest beyond the law is not a departure from democracy; it is absolutely essential to it. —Howard Zinn

WARMING

are all human beings equal?

IGNORANCE = INTOLERANCE

NO
BLOOD
FOR
OIL
www.BloodForOil.org

Revolution is not a one time event. —Audre Lorde

If you want to be a real human being – a real woman, a real man – you cannot tolerate things which put you to indignation, to outrage. You must stand up. I always say to people, 'Look around; look at what makes you unhappy, what makes you furious, and then engage yourself in some action.' —STEPHANE HESSEL

HOUSING IS A HUMAN RIGHT, NOT JUST A COMMODITY
LA VIVIENDA ES UN DERECHO, NO UN NEGOCIO
DECENT HOUSING CONDITIONS
POR UNA VIVIENDA DIGNA

Caring for myself is not self-indulgence, it is self-preservation, and that is an act of political warfare. —Audre Lorde

#SalvaLoPublico
Educación
Pública

BUDOUCNOST — FUTURE

The master's tools will never dismantle the master's house. —Audre Lorde

UNITED WAR CORPORATION

You're not to be so blind with patriotism that you can't face reality. Wrong is wrong, no matter who does it or says it. —Malcolm X

KOREA 2018

The New
Normality

I think that riots, rebellions, uprisings are not demonstrations. This is a visceral expression of rage and frustration.... —Keeanga-Yamahtta Taylor

No animals shall be exploited for the amusement of man. ARTICLE 10 / UNIVERSAL DECLARATION OF ANIMAL RIGHTS

En Guatemala, ser mujer y víctima es una misma cosa
Violada
torturada
mujeres
Atada con alambre de espinos, espantosamente mutilada, con insultos grabados sobre la piel, violada, asesinada, decapitada y tirada en un arcén. En Guatemala-capital es raro el día en que no se encuentra una mujer en estas condiciones. En 2005, la media ha sido de dos cuerpos al día: 312 hasta mayo, que se suman a las 1.500 violadas, torturadas y asesinadas en los últimos cuatro años. Queda claro que, en Guatemala, ser mujer y víctima es una misma cosa.
In Guatemala, being a woman and a victim is the same thing /// Tortured women raped murdered /// Bound with barbed wire, horribly mutilated, insults engraved into her skin, raped, murdered, beheaded, and thrown onto the side of the road. In Guatemala City, it is a rare day when a woman is not found in these conditions. In 2005, the average was two bodies a day: 312 as of May, in addition

AMNESIA
INTERNATIONAL
AGAINST TORTURE IN
ALGERIA

thanks!
nurses
caregivers
cleaning teams
doctors
medical staff
researchers
scientists
If I die, I don't want to be remembered as a hero. I want you to use it as fuel to demand change... —Nurse Emily Plerskalla

Contra
la pena
de
muerte
Against
the
death
penalty
Justice is never advanced in the taking of human life. —Coretta Scott King

Democracy is the best revenge. —Benazir Bhutto

Democracy is the best revenge. —Benazir Bhutto

THE ENEMY IS FEAR WE THINK IT IS HATE BUT IT IS REALLY FEAR

We have been raised to fear the yes within ourselves, our deepest cravings. —Audre Lorde

YES
&
NO
UNITED KINGDOM VS. EUROPEAN UNION
BREXIT 2016 UK

As I would not be a slave, so I would not be a master. This expresses my idea of democracy. —Abraham Lincoln

PEACE
NO MORE GTMO
PELIGRO
Pictopia Stencil Workshop

NO
NO PRIVATIZACIÓN
SERVICIOS LIMPIEZA
HOSPITALES
MADRID

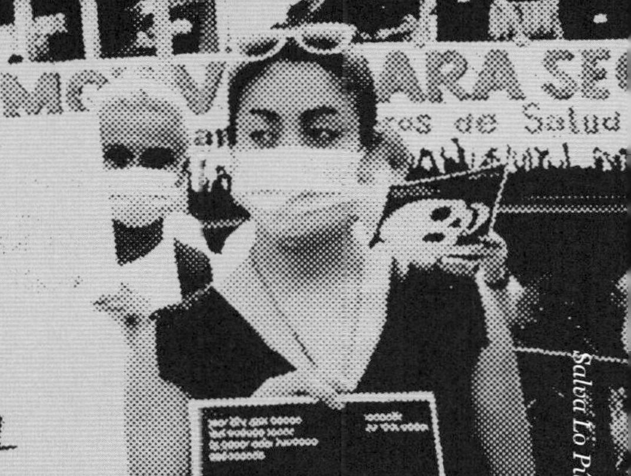
NO
SÍ

Salvà Lo Público / Sanitarios Movilizados

climate change *affects* me

445

446

447

448

449

450 *

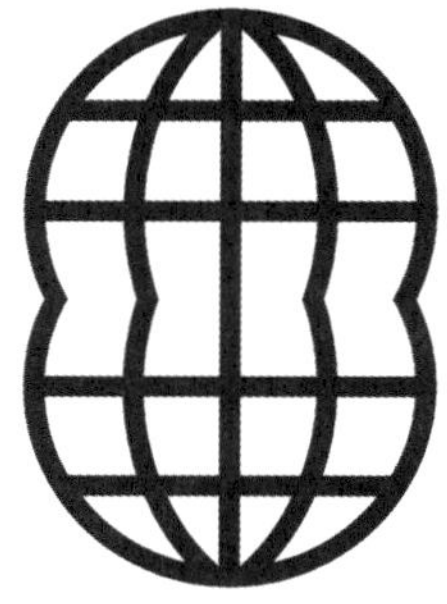

451

452

453

***The People's Climate March** /
was a large-scale activist event
orchestrated by the People's Climate
Movement in 2014 to advocate global
action against climate change.

***La Marche mondiale pour le climat** /
un événement militant à grande
échelle, organisé par People's Climate
Movement en 2014 pour promouvoir une
action mondiale contre le changement
climatique.

***La Marcha Popular por el Clima** /
fue un evento activista a gran escala
orquestado por People's Climate
Movement en 2014 para abogar por
una acción mundial contra el cambio
climático.

454

455

456

457

458 *

459

460

461

462

***Pictograms to the world** /
in the field of visual communication
design today there are many
important nonfiction subjects.
We need to collaborate and live up
to such social expectations through
pictogram design. —Yukio Ota

***Pictogrammes pour le monde** /
dans le domaine de la communication
visuelle on devrait traiter aujourd'hui
davantage de sujets liés à la réalité.
Nous devons collaborer et être partie
prenante de la société au travers
de la conception de pictogrammes.
—Yukio Ota

***Pictogramas para el mundo** /
en el campo del diseño para la
comunicación visual hay actualmente
muchos temas importantes fuera de la
ficción. Por ello, deberíamos colaborar
para responder a esas expectativas
sociales a través del diseño
de pictogramas. —Yukio Ota

463

464

465

466

467 *

468

469

470

471

***The School Strike for Climate /**
Fridays for Future (FFF), Youth for
Climate, Climate Strike, and Youth Strike
for Climate are all part of an international
movement of school children who
take time off from class on Fridays
to participate in demonstrations.

***La Grève étudiante pour le climat
ou la Grève scolaire pour le climat**
/ Fridays for Future (FFF) est un
mouvement international de collégiens
et de lycéens quittant leur établissement
scolaire le vendredi pour participer à
des manifestations en faveur de l'action
contre le réchauffement climatique.

***Huelga Escolar por el Clima /**
Viernes por el Futuro (FFF), Juventud
por el Clima, Huelga Climática o Huelga
Juvenil por el Clima, es un movimiento
internacional de escolares que los
viernes dejan de asistir a clase para
participar en manifestaciones.

472 *

473

474

475

***Nuclear Disarmament /**
in 1958, Gerald Holtom designed the symbol for the Campaign for Nuclear Disarmament (CDN). It is now known as the 'peace' symbol.

***Désarmement nucléaire /**
en 1958, Gerald Holtom a créa le symbole de la Campagne pour le Désarmement Nucléaire (CDN), qui est devenu aujourd'hui le symbole de la paix.

***Desarme Nuclear /**
en 1958 Gerald Holtom diseña el símbolo de la Campaña de Desarme Nuclear (CDN). Ahora es más conocido como el símbolo de la «paz».

476

477

GAZA
STOP
NOW

479 *

***The Second Intifada** / was a
period of intensified Israeli–Palestinian
violence in 2000, which Palestinians
describe as an uprising against Israel.
Israelis, meanwhile, consider
it a prolonged terror attack...

***La Seconde Intifada** / désigne une
période d'intensification de la violence
israélo-palestinienne à partir de 2000.
Les Palestiniens la décrivent comme un
soulèvement contre Israël ; les Israéliens,
quant à eux, comme une attaque
terroriste prolongée.

***La Segunda Intifada** / fue un período
de intensificación de la violencia israelí-
palestina en 2000, que los palestinos
describen como un levantamiento
contra Israel, mientras que los israelíes
lo consideran un terror prolongado...

480

481

482

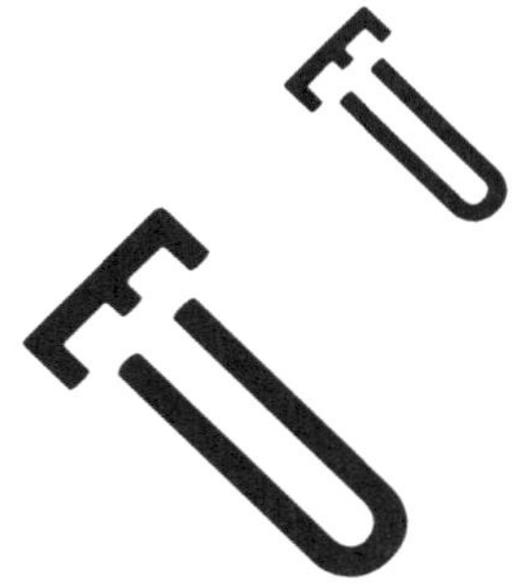

483 *

484

485

***I Am a Man** / these signs were used at the Memphis sanitation strike in 1968, as part of the Civil Rights Movement. 'I Am a Man' is a declaration of civil rights, a personal statement of independence against oppression.

***I Am a Man** / Je suis un homme (Et je mérite le respect) était un slogan utilisé par le Mouvement des droits civiques lors de la grève des éboueurs de Memphis en 1968. Une déclaration personnelle d'indépendance contre l'oppression.

***Soy un hombre** / fue un eslogan utilizado por el Movimiento de Derechos Civiles en la huelga de saneamiento de Memphis en 1968. Es una declaración personal y de independencia contra la opresión.

ALGERIA
AN OPEN-AIR PRISON
* DALILA TALEB

486 *

***Failure is impossible** / Susan B. Anthony (1820-1906) uttered these words in her final suffrage speech. Committed to social justice, she worked tirelessly to improve the lives of labourers, African Americans, and women. Her motto: 'Organize, agitate, educate, must be our war cry.'

***L'échec est impossible** / a déclaré Susan B. Anthony (1820-1906) dans son dernier discours pour le suffrage des femmes. Engagée en faveur de la justice sociale, elle s'est efforcée d'améliorer la vie des travailleurs, des Afro-Américains et des femmes. Sa devise : « Organiser, agiter, éduquer doit être notre cri de guerre ».

***Es imposible fracasar** / dijo Susan B. Anthony (1820-1906) en el discurso final del sufragio. Comprometida con la justicia social, trabajó para mejorar la vida de los trabajadores, los afroamericanos y las mujeres. Su lema: «Organizar, agitar, educar, debe ser nuestro grito de guerra» .

487

488

489

490

TOLERANCE

Originally from the Latin tolerans (present participle of tolerare; "to bear, endure, tolerate"). The word toleration was first used in English in the 1510s to mean "permission granted by authority, licence", moving towards the meaning of "forbearance, sufferance" in the 1580s. Historically, most incidents and writings pertaining to toleration involve the status of minority and dissenting viewpoints in relation to a dominant state religion. In the 20th century and after, analysis of the doctrine of toleration has been expanded to include political and ethnic groups, LGBT individuals and other minorities, while human rights embodies the principle of legally enforced toleration.

491

492 *

493

494

495

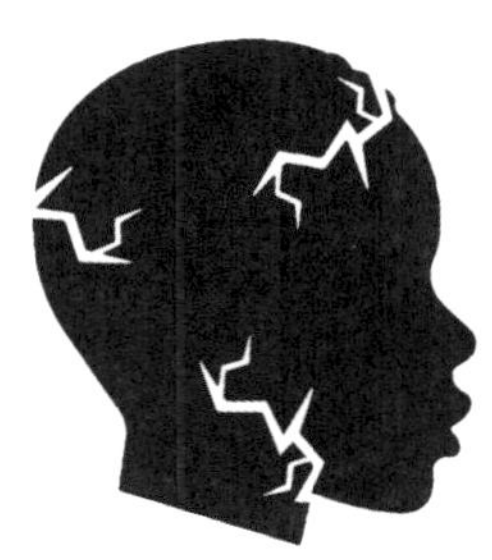

496

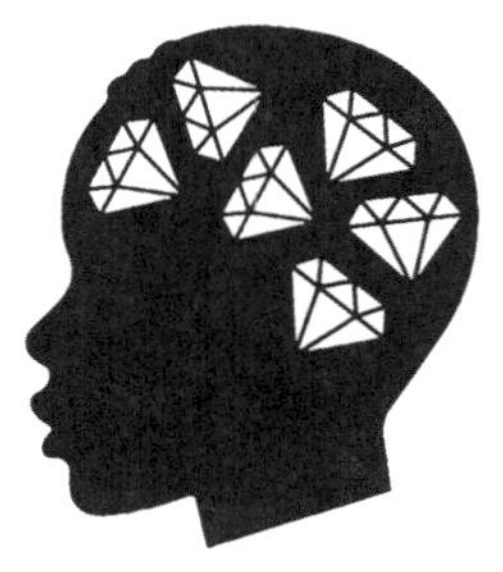

497

498

499

***Medu Art Ensemble** / was a group of 'cultural workers' who fled into exile in Gaborone, Botswana, in 1977. Medu saw its aesthetic and cultural approach as rooted in the strands of South African resistance and Africanist culture.

***Medu Art Ensemble** / était un groupe de « travailleurs culturels » qui ont fui en exil à Gaborone, au Botswana, en 1977. Medu considérait que son approche esthétique et culturelle était enracinée dans les courants de la résistance sud-africaine et de la culture africaniste.

***Medu Art Ensemble** / fue un grupo de «trabajadores culturales» que se exilió en Gaborone (Botswana) en 1977. Medu veía su enfoque estético y cultural enraizado en los hilos de la resistencia sudafricana y la cultura africanista.

500 *

***Stop de Kindermoord** /
('Stop the child murder') in the 1970s,
a citizens' group took measures against
car traffic. They occupied accident
blackspots and organized special days
where streets were closed to allow
children to play safely.

***Stop de Kindermoord** / (Arrêtez
le meurtre d'enfants) dans les années
1970, un groupe de citoyens ont pris des
mesures contre la circulation automobile.
Ils ont occupé les points noirs, sources
d'accidents fréquents, et ont organisé des
journées spéciales, pendant lesquelles les
rues étaient fermées pour permettre aux
enfants de jouer en toute sécurité.

***Stop de Kindermoord** / (Detened
el asesinato de niños) en los años
70 un grupo de ciudadanos tomó
algunas medidas contra el tráfico de
coches: ocuparon los puntos negros de
accidentes y organizaron días especiales
en los que se cerraron las calles para
permitir a los niños jugar con seguridad.

PROTEST PICTOGRAM ACTIVISM

501 *

***Provo's** 'White Bicycle Plan'
(Amsterdam 1965)

Le « White Bicycle Plan » (Plan
Bicyclette blanche) du mouvement
Provo (Amsterdam 1965)

«Plan de la Bicicleta Blanca»
Los Provos (Amsterdam 1965)

502

503

504

505

506 *

507

508

509

510

***Heroic Guerrilla Fighter** / the portrait of Che Guevara, photographed by Alberto Korda, is the symbol of the Cuban Revolution and one of the most reproduced images of the 20th century, thanks to the work of designers such as Jim Fitzpatrick and Félix Beltrán.

***Guerrillero Heroico** / le portrait de Che Guevara, photographié par Alberto Korda, est devenu le symbole de la Révolution cubaine et est l'une des icônes les plus reproduites du XXe siècle, grâce au travail de graphistes comme Jim Fitzpatrick et Félix Beltrán.

***Guerrillero Heroico** / el retrato del Che Guevara, fotografiado por Alberto Korda, es el símbolo de la Revolución Cubana y uno de los más reproducidos del siglo XX gracias al trabajo de diseñadores como Jim Fitzpatrick y Félix Beltrán.

WE HAVE NO RIGHT TO BELIEVE THAT FREEDOM CAN BE WON WITHOUT STRUGGLE
NO TENEMOS DERECHO A PENSAR QUE LA LIBERTAD PUEDE SER GANADA SIN LUCHAR

LA PALABRA
'HURACÁN' DERIVA
DEL VOCABLO MAYA
'HURAKAN',
NOMBRE DE UN DIOS CREADOR,
QUIEN, SEGÚN LOS MAYAS,
ESPARCIÓ SU ALIENTO
A TRAVÉS DE LAS CAÓTICAS
AGUAS DEL INICIO,
CREANDO, ASÍ, LA TIERRA.
'HURAKAN
KATRINA'
ECOLOGICAL
AND
HUMANITARIAN
DISASTER
THE
HURRICANE
POSTER
PROJECT

511

512

513

514

515

516

517

***Sanitarios Necesarios** /
a movement without parties or unions
that was born in 2020 to defend
a quality public health system after
the COVID-19 crisis. / **Salva Lo
Público** is a group of plastic and
visual artists in solidarity with culture,
art, and the public.

518

***Sanitarios Necesarios** /
un mouvement sans parti ni syndicat qui
est né en 2020 pour défendre un système
de santé publique de qualité après la
crise COVID-19. / **Salva Lo Público** est
un groupe d'artistes plasticiens et visuels,
exprimant leur solidarité envers la culture,
l'art et le public.

519 *

***Sanitarios Necesarios** /
movimiento sin partidos ni sindicatos
que nació en 2020 para defender
una sanidad pública de calidad tras
la crisis del Covid-19. / **Salva Lo
Público** es un colectivo de artistas
plásticos y v suales solidarios
con la cultura, el arte y lo público.

UN MUNDO FELIZ

520 *

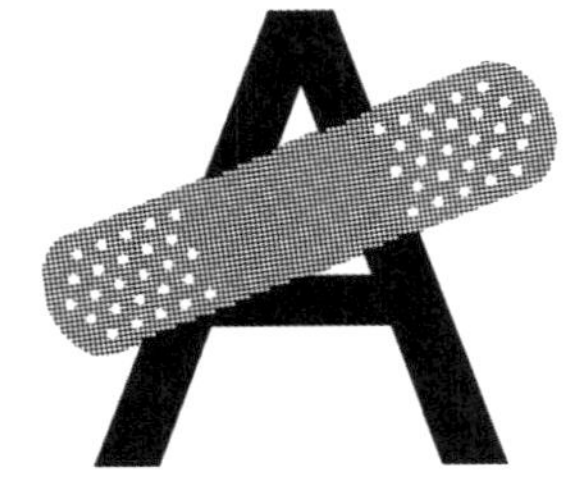

521

522

523

524

525

526

527

528

***No Blood for Oil** / this slogan featured on many a sign during the run-up to the US-led invasion of Iraq, as well as throughout the early years of the occupation as global opposition to it grew.

***No Blood for Oil** / Pas de sang pour le pétrole, ce slogan figurait sur de nombreuses pancartes pendant la période précédant l'invasion de l'Irak par les États-Unis, ainsi que durant les premières années d'occupation, où l'opposition mondiale à cette occupation s'accentuait.

***No Blood for Oil** / este eslogan apareció en muchos carteles de manifestaciones durante el período previo a la invasión de Irak liderada por los EE.UU. y en los primeros años de la ocupación a medida que crecía la oposición mundial a la misma.

529

**Protest Fonts
& Political Types**
by Manuel Ponce
& UMF

*Cómica Sans
Policía Sans
Revolution Dingbats
Stencil Mix
Type4Peace
VIHvo Font*

531

532 *

533

534

535

536

537

538

539

***Anti Nazi League** / (ANL) was an organisation set up in 1977 on the initiative of the Socialist Workers Party, with sponsorship from trade unions and the endorsement of prominent people, to oppose the rise of far-right groups in the United Kingdom.

***La Ligue Anti-Nazi** / (ANL) est une organisation britannique créée en 1977, à l'initiative du *Socialist Workers Party*, en collaboration avec les syndicats et l'appui de personnalités, afin de s'opposer à la montée des groupes d'extrême droite au Royaume-Uni.

***La Liga Antinazi** / (ANL) fue una organización creada en 1977 por el Partido Socialista de los Trabajadores, con el patrocinio de los sindicatos y el respaldo de personalidades destacadas para oponerse al surgimiento de grupos de extrema derecha en el Reino Unido.

THE TRUMP WALL

I WANT A STRONG BORDER. I DO WANT A WALL. WALLS DO WORK, YOU JUST HAVE TO SPEAK TO THE FOLKS IN ISRAEL. WALLS WORK IF THEY'RE PROPERLY CONSTRUCTED. I KNOW HOW TO BUILD, BELIEVE ME, I KNOW HOW TO BUILD. – DONALD TRUMP / PRESIDENT OF THE UNITED STATES

VOTE
MUTE
GAG LAW — LEY MORDAZA

AUSCHWITZ
AUSCHWITZ
AUSCHWITZ
AUSCHWITZ
AUSCHWI
SCHWITZ
HALT!
AUSCHWITZ
AUSCHWI
SCH

There is a source of power in each of us that we don't realize until we take responsibility. —Diane Nash

Il y a une source d'énergie en chacun de nous, dont nous ne prenons pas conscience tant que nous n'avons pas pris nos responsabilités —Diane Nash

Hay una fuente de poder en cada uno de nosotros de la que no nos damos cuenta hasta que asumimos la responsabilidad. —Diane Nash

BIG
DRE
AM
MY FEAR
WAS NOT
OF DEATH
ITSELF BUT
A DEATH
WITH
MEAN
TRUE
LIFE
IS NO
REAL

76   Peuple / Banques.

80   Droits civils, droits de l'homme / Le 25 octobre 2005, Rosa Parks, surnommée « mère du mouvement des droits civiques » est décédée. Elle a changé le cours de l'histoire américaine en refusant, en 1955, de céder sa place dans un bus à un homme blanc.

81   Mon choix.

87   Cibles du terrorisme.

100   Le Guatemala a le troisième taux de féminicides le plus élevé du monde / Entre 2014 et 2016, il y a eu 2 264 morts violentes de femmes au Guatemala, dont 611 ont été déclarées officiellement féminicides. Durant cette période, 59 responsables de ces assassinats ont été incarcérés. Il s'agit un problème caché et, en tant que société, nous devons redoubler d'efforts en termes d'information, de sensibilisation et de formation afin que les femmes prennent conscience qu'elles ne doivent pas être victimes de ces violences.

108   Incendie et reconstruction / La cathédrale Notre-Dame de Paris, lundi 15 avril 2019.

113   La vie des noirs compte / Black Lives Matter est une des cibles centrales de la désinformation et vous êtes une ligne de défense essentielle.

120   L'incarcération n'est pas une peine qui favorise l'égalité des chances.

131   « C'est mon corps, c'est mon choix ».

136   *Errorisme (Error en anglais signifie erreur) / T*(errorism) / Une fin de la terreur est préférable à une terreur sans fin. — Sophie Scholl.

137   Politique : « Poli » provenant du grec et signifiant plusieurs et « tique » signifiant une créature suceuse de sang. – Robin Williams.

141   Ne laissez pas la peur étouffer votre voix ! « Shut up! The voice of democracy in danger » (Taisez-vous ! La voix de la démocratie en danger) est une réaction à la mort choquante du journaliste slovaque Jan Kuciak et de sa fiancée, Martina Kushnihova, en février 2018. En tant que journaliste, Jan Kuciak s'est surtout penché sur les enquêtes relatives à la fraude fiscale, impliquant plusieurs hommes d'affaires ayant des liens avec des politiciens slovaques de haut rang.

148   Nous devons nous mettre en colère et comprendre ce qui est en jeu. Puis transformer cette colère en action pour agir à l'unisson et ne jamais abandonner. — Greta Thunberg.

151   Il y a une situation d'urgence et de catastrophe naturelle en iran / les inondations du golestan / 19 mars 2019.

165   Meurtre, honneur et liberté de la presse / Censure assassine.

166   Une seule voie / Une société qui place l'égalité devant la liberté se trouvera dépourvue de l'une et de l'autre. Une société qui place la liberté devant l'égalité se retrouvera avec une bonne dose des deux. — Milton Friedman.

169   Le Sahara libre / Agir maintenant pour défendre les droits de l'homme au sahara occidental.

166   Crimée / Ukraine 2014.

173   Je pense qu'une révolte ici et là est une bonne chose, et aussi nécessaire dans le monde politique que les tempêtes dans le monde physique. — Thomas Jefferson.

174   Nous n'aurons jamais une société si nous détruisons l'environnement. — Margaret Mead.

175   Le militant n'est pas celui qui dit que la rivière est sale. Le militant est l'homme qui nettoie la rivière. — Ross Perot.

176   Le domicile est l'endroit le plus dangereux pour les femmes. / Le 25 novembre, journée internationale pour l'élimination de la violence à l'égard des femmes.

177   Je ne suis pas libre tant que les femmes ne sont pas libres, même si leurs chaînes sont très différentes des miennes. — Audre Lorde.

178   Indignez-vous ! / Spanish Revolution / Pour moi, la démocratie véritable et authentique émergera lorsque les groupes privilégiés aideront les groupes non privilégiés à devenir plus privilégiés. — Stéphane Hessel.

179   Les peuples ne devraient pas avoir peur de leurs gouvernements. Les gouvernements devraient avoir peur du peuple. — Alan Moore, V pour Vendetta.

180   Je ne veux pas de l'art pour quelques uns, pas plus que je ne veux de l' éducation pour quelques-uns, ou de la liberté pour quelques-uns. — William Morris.

181   L'instruction est comme la liberté : elle ne se donne pas, elle se prend. — Jacques Rancière.

182   Stop à l'expulsion / le logement pour les gens, pas pour le profit ! La plate-forme des victimes du crédit hypothécaire (PAH) action pour le droit au logement / L'activisme commence avec vous, la démocratie commence avec vous. Bougez, Agissez ! Ah vous voilà. — Thom Hartmann.

183   Avertissement / Protester en dehors des limites prescrites par la loi, ce n'est pas combattre la démocratie. Cela lui est, au contraire, absolument essentiel. — Howard Zinn.

184   Les adultes répètent sans cesse qu'ils ont une dette envers les jeunes, qu'il faut leur donner de l'espoir. Mais je ne veux pas de votre espoir. Je veux que vous paniquiez. — Greta Thunberg.

185   Les êtres humains sont-ils tous égaux ? / Ignorance = intolérance.

186   Pas de sang pour le pétrole.

187   Fraternité, liberté, égalité, inhumanité / La révolution n'est pas un événement ponctuel. — Audre Lorde.

188   Si vous voulez être un véritable être humain - une vraie femme, un vrai homme - vous ne pouvez pas tolérer ce qui vous indigne, ce qui vous révolte. Vous devez réagir. Je dis toujours aux gens : « Regardez autour de vous ; regardez ce qui vous rend malheureux, ce qui vous rend furieux et, ensuite, engagez-vous dans une action. — Stéphane Hessel.

189   Le logement est un droit, pas une marchandise ! / Des conditions de logememt décentes.

190   Prendre soin de soi n'est pas de l'égocentrisme, c'est de l'auto-préservation, et c'est un acte de combat politique. — Audre Lorde.

191   Campagne de défense de l'éducation publique / Sauve Le Public.

193   Les outils du maître ne démantèleront jamais la maison du maître. — Audre Lorde.

194   Corporations guerrières unies / Tu ne dois pas être si aveugle de patriotisme que tu ne peux pas faire face à la réalité. Le mal est mal, peu importe qui le fait ou le dit. — Malcolm X.

196   La Nouvelle Normalité / Je pense que les émeutes, les rébellions, les soulèvements ne sont pas des manifestations. C'est une expression viscérale de la rage et de la frustration. — Keeanga-Yamahtta Taylor.

197   Nul animal ne doit être exploité pour le divertissement de l'homme. / Article 10 de la Déclaration Universelle des Droits de l'Animal.

199   Amnésie Internationale Contre la Torture en Algérie.

200   Merci ! ux infirmières, au personnel soignant, aux équipes de nettoyage, aux docteurs, au personnel médical, aux chercheurs, aux scientifiques / Si je meurs, je ne veux pas qu'on se souvienne de moi comme d'un héros. Je veux que vous utilisiez ma mort comme un carburant pour exiger des changements. — Infirmière Emily Pierskalla.

201   Contre la peine de mort / On ne sert jamais la justice en prenant une vie humaine. — Coretta Scott King.

202   La démocratie est la meilleure des vengeances. — Benazir Bhutto.

203   L'ennemi c'est la peur, on croit que c'est la haine, mais en réalité c'est la peur / Nous avons été élevés à craindre le « oui » en nous, nos désirs les plus enfouis. — Audre Lorde.

205   De même que je ne voudrais pas être un esclave, je ne voudrais pas être un maître. Telle est ma conception de la démocratie. — Abraham Lincoln.

208   Le changement climatique m'affecte aussi.

217   Algérie : une prison à ciel ouvert.

220   « To bear, endure, tolerate » (supporter, endurer, tolérer) vient du latin *tolerans* (participe présent de *tolerare*). Le mot tolérance a été utilisé pour la première fois en anglais vers 1510 pour signifier une « permission accordée par l'autorité, une licence », pour se rapprocher du sens de « forbearance, sufferance » (tolérance,

patience, endurance) dans les années
1580. Historiquement, la plupart des
incidents et des écrits relatifs à la
tolérance concernent le statut des points
de vue minoritaires et dissidents par
rapport à une religion d'État dominante.
Depuis le XXe siècle, l'analyse de la
doctrine de tolérance a été élargie pour
inclure les groupes politiques et ethniques,
les personnes LGBT, les individus et
d'autres minorités, tandis que les droits
de l'homme incarnent le principe de
tolérance appliqué légalement.

225 Nous n'avons pas le droit de croire
que la liberté peut être acquise sans
combattre.

226 L'ouragan Katrina : un désastre
écologique et humanitaire / Le Projet
d'Affiche Ouragan.

232 Le mur de Trump / Je veux une
frontière forte. Je veux un mur. Les murs
fonctionnent, vous n'avez qu'à demander
aux gens en israel. Les murs fonctionnent
s'ils sont bien construits. Je sais comment
le construire, croyez-moi, je sais comment
le construire. — Donald Trump, président
des États-Unis.

233 Votez en silence / Loi du bâillon.

CARTELES: UNA TRADUCCIÓN

64   La cuestión migratoria.

76   Personas / Bancos.

81   25 de octubre de 2005. Rosa Parks,
la mujer conocida como «la madre de los
movimientos por los derechos civiles»,
ha muerto. Parks cambió el curso de la
historia de EE.UU. cuando en 1955 se
negó a ceder su asiento en un autobús
a un hombre blanco.

81   Mi elección.

100   Guatemala tiene el tercer índice
más alto de feminicidio del mundo / Entre
2014 y 2016 hubo 2264 muertes violentas
de mujeres en Guatemala, de las cuales
611 fueron reportadas formalmente como
feminicidios. En ese mismo periodo
fueron encarcelados 59 perpetradores.
Es un problema oculto y la sociedad
debe trabajar más en las labores de
información, concienciación y formación
para que las mujeres se den cuenta de
que no deberían sufrir abusos.

113   Black Lives Matter es un objetivo
central de ataques de desinformación
y tú eres una pieza clave en su defensa.

136   (T)errorismo / Es preferible el fin del
terror a un terror sin fin. — Sophie Scholl.

137   Politics: *poli*, palabra latina que
significa «muchos» y «tics» que significa
«criaturas chupasangre» [en inglés, *tick*,
«garrapata»]. — Robin Williams.

145   ¡No dejes que el miedo apague tu
voz! «¡Cállate! La voz de la democracia
en peligro» es una reacción a la trágica
muerte del periodista eslovaco Jan
Kuciak y su novia, Martina Kusnirova
en febrero de 2018. Como reportero,
Kuciak se dedicaba a investigar los

fraudes fiscales de varios empresarios
con conexiones con políticos eslovacos
de primer nivel.

148   Tenemos que enfadarnos y
comprender lo que está en juego.
Y después, necesitamos transformar el
enfado en acción y mantenernos unidos
y no rendirnos jamás. — Greta Thunberg.

151   Hay un estado de emergencia
y de desastre natural en Irán.

165   Asesinato, honor y libertad de
prensa: censura mortal.

166   Sentido único / Una sociedad
que antepone la igualdad a la libertad
no tendrá ninguna de las dos.
Una sociedad que antepone la libertad
a la igualdad conseguirá ambas en alto
grado. — Milton Friedman.

173   Sostengo que una pequeña
revolución es buena de vez en cuando
y que es tan necesaria en el mundo
político como las tormentas en el físico.
— Thomas Jefferson.

174   No tendremos sociedad si
destruimos el entorno. – Margaret Mead.

175   El activista no es el hombre que
dice que el río está sucio. El activista es
el hombre que lo limpia. — Ross Perot.

176   El hogar es el sitio más peligroso
para las mujeres.

177   No soy libre mientras haya una
mujer que no sea libre, incluso aunque
sus cadenas sean muy distintas de las
mías. — Audre Lorde.

178   Para mí, la verdadera democracia se
produce cuando los grupos privilegiados
ayudan a los no privilegiados a adquirir
privilegios. — Stéphane Hessel.

179   El pueblo no debería temer a
su gobierno. Los gobiernos deberían
temer a sus pueblos. — Alan Moore,
V de Vendetta.

180   No quiero arte para unos pocos,
lo mismo que no quiero educación para
unos pocos, ni libertad para unos pocos.
— William Morris.

181   La educación es como la libertad,
no se da: se toma. – Jacques Rancière.

182   El activismo empieza por ti, la
democracia empieza por ti, ¡Sal ahí afuera!,
¡Actúa! Te toca a ti. — Thom Hartmann.

183   Protestar contra la ley no es
apartarse de la democracia: es algo
absolutamente esencial para ella.
— Howard Zinn.

184   Los adultos dicen que tienen el deber
de dar esperanza a los jóvenes. Pero yo
no quiero vuestra esperanza. Yo quiero
que tengáis pánico. — Greta Thunberg.

185   ¿Son iguales todos los seres
humanos? / Ignorancia = intolerancia

186   Sangre a cambio de petróleo, no.

187   La revolución no es un
acontecimiento irrepetible. — Audre Lorde.

188   Si quieres ser un ser humano,
un hombre o una mujer de verdad, no
puedes tolerar las cosas que te indignan
y te ultrajan. Tienes que alzarte. Siempre
le digo a la gente: «mirad a vuestro

alrededor, a lo que os hace infelices,
a lo que os enfurece, y después
poneos en acción.» — Stéphane Hessel.

190   Cuidar de mí misma no es auto-
indulgencia, es autopreservación y es
un acto de lucha política. — Audre Lorde.

193   Las herramientas del amo
nunca desmantelarán la casa del amo.
— Audre Lorde.

194   El patriotismo no puede cegarte
e impedirte ver la realidad. Lo que está
mal está mal, no importa quién lo haga
o lo diga. — Malcolm X.

196   Creo que los disturbios, las
rebeliones, los alzamientos no son
demostraciones. Son expresiones
viscerales de rabia y frustración...
— Keeanga-Yamahtta Taylor.

197   Ningún animal debe ser explotado
para la diversión del hombre.
Artículo 10. Declaración Universal
de los Derechos de los Animales.

199   Contra la tortura en Argelia.

200   ¡Gracias! Enfermeras, cuidadoras,
equipos de limpieza, doctoras, personal
médico, investigadores, científicos /
Si muero, no quiero que me recuerden
como a una heroína. Quiero que uséis
mi muerte como energía para pedir el
cambio... — Emily Pierskalla, enfermera.

201   La justicia nunca avanza tomando
vidas humanas. — Coretta Scott King.

202   La democracia es la mejor venganza.
— Benazir Bhutto.

203   El enemigo es el miedo. Creemos
que es el odio, pero en realidad es miedo /
Nos han educado para temer el sí que
llevamos dentro, nuestros anhelos más
profundos. — Audre Lorde.

205   No quiero ser esclavo, lo mismo que
no quiero ser amo. Esto expresa mi idea
de la democracia. — Abraham Lincoln.

208   El cambio climático me afecta a mí.

220   Tolerancia. Derivado del latín *tolerans*
(participio presente de *tolerare*, «soportar,
aguantar, tolerar»). La palabra *toleration*
fue empleada por primera vez en inglés
en 1510 para indicar «permiso concedido
por la autoridad, licencia» y hacia 1580
había evolucionado a «aceptación,
consentimiento». Históricamente, la
mayoría de las incidencias y escritos
alusivos a tolerancia aluden al estatus de
minorías y a puntos de vista divergentes
con relación a una religión estatal
dominante. En el siglo XX y después, el
análisis de la doctrina de la tolerancia se
ha ampliado para incluir a grupos políticos
y étnicos, personas LGTB y otras minorías,
y os derechos humanos incluyen el
principio de tolerancia defendida por la ley.

232   El Muro de Trump / Quiero una
frontera fuerte. Quiero un muro. Los muros
funcionan, preguntadle a la gente de
Israel. Los muros funcionan si están bien
construidos; creedme, yo sé construir.
— Donald Trump, Presidente de
los Estados Unidos de América.

233   Vota / Calla.

THANKS

Félix Beltrán, Raquel Pelta, Josh MacPhee, Alain Le Quernec, Teresa Sdralevich, Pekka Loiri, Liz McQuiston, Steven Heller, Bettina Richter, Experimental Jetset, Avram Finkelstein, Sarah Corbett, Alejandro Magallanes, Thomas Lemahieu (*l'Humanité*), Fons Hickmann, Lincoln Cushing, King ADZ, Jordi Claramonte, Tom Bieling, Steve Lambert, Natalia Mirapeix Bedia, Yukio Ota, Andrea Rauch, David Tartakover, Timothy Samara, Isidro Ferrer, Óscar Mariné, Miguel Ángel Pacheco, Manuel Ponce, Isabel García, Milton Glasser / Mirko Ilic, Josua Berger / PLAZM, Jonathan Barnbrook, KennardPhillipps, Sébastien Marchal, Manuel Estrada, Mykola Kovalenko, El Fantasma de Heredia, Patrick Thomas, Byoung Choi, Coco Cerella, Ruedi & Vera Baur (*Design2Context*), Interference Archive, Lita Talarico, Susan Buck-Morss, Martha Rosler, Aaris Sherin, Antoni Muntadas, Miguel Trillo, Natalia Volpe y Gabriel Mahia (*Onaire*), Natalia / Paco (*Minchó*), Mireia / Alberto (*Makea Tu Vida*), Pablo España (*Democracia*), Luis García (*ILC*), Javier Panera (*DA2*), Vera Brito (*MUDE*), AtypI (*Helsinki 2005*), Tania / Rafael / Agustín / Kore / Raquel / Kistine (*MUSAC*), c arte c (*UCM*), Juan Ra / Marga (*La Sexta*), Lucía Zapata (UP&UP), La Galería de Magdalena, Ofelio Serpa, Cristina Hernánz, Kevin McCourt, Rafa Iglesias (*Ediciones de Ruina*), Oswaldo Terreros (*Movimiento GRSB*), Sara / Jaime / Ana / Beatriz (*Dfest*), Candela / Fernando / Lalo / Toes (*Barriopajeros + Autoedita o muere*), Lucía Casanova, David Gil, Nacho Clemente, Vicius (*Sistema de Monos*), Sara Martínez (*Las Angustias*), Mª J. Bonafonte / Bea Brugarolas, Verónica de la Sierra, Yetta Aguado Arnold, Héctor (*Graffather*), Miguel Anxo Pena, Pep Carrió, Borja Blanco / Alberto Hernández, Nora / Pablo (*TypoMad*), Ana Torralba, Malagón, Álvaro R. G, Jaume Pujagut, Mª Àngels Fortea Castillo, Juan Cardosa, Maria Papaefstathiou, Carol A. Wells (*Center of the Study of Political Graphics*), Clara Hatton Gallery, Hervé Matine (*Poster for Tomorrow*), MUMEDI, Occupy + Occuprint, Emzin Institut Seminar, Positive Posters, Good 50x70 / Trienal di Milano, School of Visual Arts NY, DOX / Centre for Contemporary Art, CCE Montevideo, Martin Luther King Jr. Center NY, Start Soma Gallery, Non-Breaking Space, ar/ge kunst Gallery, Public Space One, Internationale Politische Plakate Leipzig, Green Patriot Posters, Recetas Urbanas, Educactivistas, Art Aero Rap, Aula Abierta, José & Cristina (*Graphicbook*), Pablo Martínez (*Espacio_E*), Carlos / Carmen / Raúl / Mariana / Mónica / César / Gaspar / Alberto / Ignacio / Mario / Lourdes... (*Salva Lo Público*), Inés Corral y Diana Paullet (*Expo Mónguer*), Anna Roig (*godArt Lab*), Anna Treska-Siwoń (*Strajk Kobiet*), Leonidas Martín, Joaquín, Silvia, Claudia (*Promopress & Hoaki*), Nora García Nieves / Tings Chak (*The Tricontinental*), Blanca Sotos (*marca blanca press*), Iva Vladimirova Vitkova & 2B, Galfano / Fernando / Javier (*UMF project*) ...

—

Felicísima Jiménez (2020)
Pablo Díaz (2019)
Frank Memmelsdorf (2017)
in memoriam

To all the collaborators and participants of Pictopia '18, Bastard Art Review, and the workshops, exhibitions, and meetings on visual activism held over the past 20 years. /

À tous les collaborateurs et participants de Pictopia '18, Bastard Art Review, et aux ateliers, expositions et réunions sur l'activisme visuel, organisés au cours de ces 20 dernières années. /

A todos los colaboradores y participantes de Pictopia'18, Bastard Art Review, de los talleres, exposiciones y encuentros de activismo visual celebrados en estos últimos 20 años.

Workshops:
Intifada gráfica: activismo gráfico, Mensaje en una botella, Diseñar es opinar, Re-vuelta: taller de agitación gráfica, Pictopía Stencil, Plátano de Canallas: autoedición y agitación visual, Letras con mensaje, Antitaller experimental, Diseño Samizdat: un diseño parlamentario, Disechos: del diseño al hecho, MemeLab'17, Re-vuelta, Pictopanic Hardware, Wallpaper Project, Lletres de Velluters, Diseñar para molestar: taller de arte social, Placer-política, PictoPower: taller de activismo visual, Sport et Racisme: pictogrammes, Mujer-desigualdad: Colectivo Montevideo, El color del cuerpo Selfie Art, PictoPower o el arte del pictomontaje: Social media addiction, Woman Sans, FakeMemeFest: foto(zine)matón
—
All the love in the world to our bold students for:
Dfest
Autoeditaomuere
PDF / Public Design Fest
Transvisible Zine
Expo Mónguer
Toguchi & Naguchi
2Bzine / PHzine
Supergráfico Fest
@ponteguape_posters

✊ ✌ ☺ ☠ 🌐 ★
unmundofeliz@gmail.com

Pangráfica Sticker Experience

Buttons, flyers, posters, postcards, T-shirts
and books. How primitive are the means
we have to dissent. And yet I believe these
modest tools can help change history.
—Milton Glaser

Boutons, dépliants, affiches, cartes postales,
T-shirts et livres. Comme ils sont primitifs,
les moyens dont nous disposons pour nous
opposer. Et pourtant, je crois que ces modestes
outils peuvent contribuer à changer l'histoire.
—Milton Glaser

Chapas, folletos, carteles, postales, camisetas
y libros. Qué primitivos son los medios
que tenemos para disentir. Y aún así creo que
estas modestas herramientas pueden ayudar
a cambiar la historia. —Milton Glaser

Strajk Kobiet movement (Poland)

PEOPLE
EL ZOO
NO MOLA
PEOPLE
BANKS
BANKS